"Delightfully playful. . . . There are few artists who can look back in contentment at a career that has spanned so many decades. . . . Between Paul Simon's songwriting and Mr. Garfunkel's skill at weaving his tenor into vocal harmonies, they have eclipsed even their original inspiration, the Everly Brothers, as the most celebrated pop music duo of all time." —*The Wall Street Journal*

"Poetic musings on a life well-lived—one that is still moving forward, always creating, always luminous." —*Bookreporter*

"[A] singular mixture of verse, doggerel, blog and diary entries, soul-baring confession, and lists of hundreds of books read . . . allowing readers to gaze into the poetic soul of an artist." —*Kirkus Reviews*

"At an early age, Garfunkel wowed his classmates, including Paul Simon, with the voice of an angel. . . . [Garfunkel] presents . . . an impressionistic, lyrical, and sometimes whimsical take on fame, singing, and aging. . . . Sensitive, soulful, sharp-tongued, and serious." —*Booklist*

"Give[s] one a real sense of who Garfunkel is as an artist and a person. . . . Fans will surely be interested in the insights on his life and work. It's a good read." —*Goldmine*

Art Garfunkel

What Is It All but Luminous

Art Garfunkel attended Columbia College and earned a master's degree in mathematics from Columbia University. With Paul Simon he was the recipient of six Grammys and the Grammy Lifetime Achievement Award; together they were inducted into the Rock & Roll Hall of Fame in 1990. He also had a successful career as an actor, appearing in many films, including *Carnal Knowledge*. Garfunkel lives in New York City with his wife, actress Kathryn Luce, and their two children. He performs around the world.

Also by Art Garfunkel

Still Water

What Is It All but Luminous

What Is It All but Luminous

Notes from an Underground Man

Art Garfunkel

Vintage Books
A Division of Penguin Random House LLC
New York

THIS BOOK IS DEDICATED TO KATHRYN,
MY WOMAN, MY WIFE.

I remember when I almost lost you.
It was 1996, James Arthur was six.
We went to Canada with hope of a
    cancer treatment.

I contemplated losing you. Losing my lover.
Raising James without you.

I couldn't handle it. It was my absolute darkest
    hour—the deepest saddest trough I ever knew.
Thinking there might be no mother, no You
    in our lives, I felt the huge Something you are.
As big as my life.

But you are here,
    in all your magnificent mystical Substantiality.

Mom was right—God is good

10/13/16

What Is It All but Luminous

With my brother Jules in back
of our house in Queens, 1949

1

I was a nervous wreck as I packed my things in the middle of the night on January 2, 1969. There in my exposed-brick bachelor apartment on East Sixty-eighth Street, I was leaving the life of four years of a girl-chasing studio rat— a life of global good fortune—to cast my fate among actors. As a music star with no acting experience, I was acutely aware that I was cross-hopping professions. Yes the Panavision movie camera is like the Neumann microphone (little things are so magnified) but how would I be received in Mexico among first-rate actors on a social level—amongst Alan Arkin, Jon Voight, Orson Welles? I quivered with insecurity as I prepared to fly, the next day, into Mike Nichols's third feature film, his follow-up to *Who's Afraid of Virginia Woolf?* and *The Graduate*—the World War II black comedy *Catch-22*.

*

Why did Mike cast me to play Captain Nately, the innocent? What about my famous singing partner? These are things I didn't ask myself.

Innately I felt the rightness of strengthening my half of Simon and Garfunkel. Paul was the writer. Paul played guitar. I was the singer, co-producer of the records, waiting for the songs to be written to start our fifth, our last album. In my mind, I played the underdog. I remember Paul being considered for a role in the movie. Or to rephrase—both of us were cast, Paul was dropped. Musicians don't talk. We were too hip to share out loud hurt feelings inside. No one begrudged Ringo when he sang "They're gonna put me in the movies." It was held in affection. Mike knew it was my right to expect the same. Recall, he once also had a brilliant partner. In May of '69, Mike took the film to Rome, and Paul's writing changed from "I know your part'll go fine"—words of a deep friendship ("The Only Living Boy in New York")—to "Why don't you write me?"—words of frustration.

*

I have these vocal cords. Two. They have vibrated with the love of sound since I was five and began to sing with the sense of God's gift running through me. In the sixth grade I made a friend who added sexy guitar rhythms and vocal harmony to my singing. We were twelve at the birth of rock 'n' roll. In our twenties we made a few special recordings. They delighted our ears and those around the world. I put my name and copyright to these lovely things.

Why didn't I write him?

No doubt Paul and I enriched each other's lives immeasurably. Where could the crazy notion come from of moving on from this wonderful duo? From hurt. From crazy motion. If Paul felt Mike had given me the means to "sock it to him," maybe I was doing just that. Why didn't I write him? Who are these two sensitive Jewish boys whose mothers loved them so much? Who throws the stone and who throws the return stone? Whose stone is imagined? Whose real?

*

I grew up near Jewel Avenue and Main Street in the borough of Queens in New York, the middle child of three boys. Hitler was winning in '41, but Rose and Jack brought home a child to their new brick house in Kew Gardens Hills. Halfway between Jamaica and Forest Hills high schools, the houses were semi-attached, with driveways between and garages in back, next to 10' x 30' grass yards. Punch ball was king. Twelve of us boys played in the street. "Car," someone called to constantly punctuate our games. My big brother Jules, Ira Landess, Bobby, Dicky Schwartz, Joel Gladstone, Michael Davidson, Henry Heitner—we played running bases, red light—green light, giant steps, hide-and-seek, two-hand touch football.

I was down the manhole, into the sewer, many
times, retrieving the Spaldeen. We flipped baseball
cards, rode our bikes (stood on the handlebars).
We caught fireflies, Japanese beetles, washed above
the wrists for dinner—we called it supper—played
chess by day and watched the Brooklyn Dodgers
at night on TV, all on our screened-in porches.
Night games were new; the Dodgers played under
the lights, in white satin. Duke Snider looked
good. But Stan Musial was the quiet king to me.

*

The picture of a boy under overcoats
    on a screened-in porch in a thunderstorm.
He brings his chair to the edge of where
    rain invades,
        closer to the lightning and the spray.

He is a stowaway.

*

We lived in the lower middle class. My dad
constructed a drop-leaf table for me, in my
bedroom with the blue linoleum floor. Brother
Jerome was down the hall. We drank Starlac and
Alba (fake watered milk) before school; a soft-
boiled egg was stirred into it. Little disgusting
flecks of albumen floated at the top. Life was
meant to be a little awful. So God created

My parents, Rose and Jack, married
October 2, 1936

Hebrew school. My Jewish training was not at
all about five thousand years of religious belief.
Who knows what the Jews believe? Keeping us
off the playground after school? It was about
the boredom of reading, of sounding out those
characters without knowing the meaning of the

words, about hearing the words from the back of a class, with the visor of my cap pulled low over my closed eyes. AND ABOUT SINGING THEM.

*

At nine I was singing Nat Cole's "Too Young" in the grade school talent shows. I played Stephen Foster in a school play and sang. Paul Simon, my schoolmate, must have been watching. I didn't know him yet; nor did I know the effect I was having on the girls, with my singing. But I knew in the synagogue, in the high-ceilinged temple room with the resounding wood walls, that my singing those minor-key, age-old prayerful melodies was moving grown men to tears in the aisles before me. Paul says it was SRO at my bar mitzvah.

*

You can't discover fuchsia twice

*

It was only in private that I learned to sing.
History misses everything.
Mites under microscopes wait till the lab
    lights are out, with no scientist keeping tab.

Everything waits to be unnoticed.
All that's recorded was played for the show.

Even Einstein applauded the brilliant minds
  smarter than his that nobody finds.

The truth is within, the compensation's
  manifest.
Napoleon's grandeur—the inner unrest.

*

Dad, Mom, Jules, Jerome, Arthur, 1949

I met Paul Simon at our graduation play, backstage in *Alice in Wonderland*. We were moving on to junior high. He was the White Rabbit (late for that date). I was the Cheshire Cat. He was FUN-NY. He started to crack me up, and we have been suppressing giggles all our lives. To him, I was the blond kid who sang. To me, he was the turned-on kid in the neighborhood, the son of a bass-playing bandleader, who moved to our neighborhood from Newark. Like Dean in *Rebel Without a Cause* he played the fringe.

*

Singing is a tickle in the back of the throat, a flutter of the abdomen, the vocal cords, called vibrato. It's sent from God through the heart, and it is un-analyzable. Some people can just do it. They listen to the radio and begin to emulate. At five or six, I was doing the inspirational songs that I heard, like "You'll Never Walk Alone." I heard my parents singing "Bye Bye Blackbird" in the living room—in two-part harmony. That I could do it too was a delight that took me to places where echo put tails on my notes—lovely extensions of sound. I fell in love with the magnifying effect of tiled rooms, hallways, and stairwells. When no one was listening, I sought to make beautiful vowel sounds for my own ears' sake. It was my private joy. Walking in rhythm over sidewalk cracks, I sang my tune. Then did it again in the next higher key. I was on my way to first grade.

Write the poem out loud
Authorize the heart
Burn the Bridge and
Be the work of art

*

My singing was a serious gift that I respected
all through my childhood, my life. I was skinny,
a lefty, a Scorpio. My father called me "Whitey
Skeeziks" but I identified with the "A" of Arthur.
It was steeple-shaped, upward aspiring, hands in
prayer. I loved my white satin collar when I sang
in the temple. I was the angel singer and I felt
"touched."

*

I went for the songs that had the goose bumps.
"If I Loved You," from *Carousel,* did it for me,
Nat Cole's wonderfully different "Nature Boy."
And I went to singers I just knew could sing:
How easy was Bing Crosby's "I'm dreaming of a
white Christmas." How brunette smooth was Jo
Stafford's "Fly the ocean in a silver plane." How
open-throated Sam Cooke's "You Send Me." How
extraordinary "It's Not for Me to Say" (Johnny
Mathis). I saw Little Richard at the Brooklyn
Paramount in '55 stand on the piano in a purple
cape. He ripped through "Long Tall Sally" and
took the night. I fell for the great groove
records. "Whole Lotta Shakin' Goin' On" had it

(Jerry Lee Lewis). So did "Don't Ya Just Know It" (Huey "Piano" Smith). Frankie Ford's "Won't you let me take you on a Sea Cruise" was as good as it got for me.

*

On Saturday mornings, in 1953, in Keds sneakers, white on white, I took my basketball to P.S. 165. We played half-court ball, three on three. Or else I listened to Martin Block's *Make Believe Ballroom* on the radio. I loved to chart the top thirty songs. It was the numbers that got me. I kept meticulous lists—when a new singer like Tony Bennett came onto the charts with "Rags to Riches," I watched the record jump from, say, #23 to #14 in a week. The mathematics of the jumps went to my sense of fun. I was commercially aware through the Hit Parade, as well as involved in the music. Johnnie Ray's "Cry," the Crewcuts' "Sh-Boom," Roy Hamilton ballads, "Unchained Melody" reached me. Soon the Everly Brothers would take me for The Big Ride.

*

As I entered Parsons Junior High where the tough kids were, Paul Simon became my one and only friend. We saw each other's uniqueness. We smoked our first cigarettes. We had retreated from all other kids. And we laughed. I opened

my school desk one day in 1954 and saw a note
from Ira Green to a friend: "Listen to the radio
tonight, I have a dedication to you." I became
aware that Alan Freed had taken this subversive
music from Cleveland to New York City. He read
dedications from teenage lovers before playing
"Earth Angel," "Sincerely." When he played
Little Richard's "Rip It Up," he left the studio

Art, Bobby, Jules on Schwinn bicycles, 1955

mic open enough to hear him pounding a stack of telephone books to the backbeat. This was no Martin Block.

Maybe I was in the land of payola, of "back alley enterprise" and pill-head disc jockeying, but what I felt was that Alan Freed loved us kids to dance, romance, and fall in love, and the music would send us. It sent me for life. It was rhythm and blues. It was black. It was from New Orleans, Chicago, Philadelphia. It was dirty music (read "sexual"). One night Alan Freed called it "rock 'n' roll." Hip was born for me. Chuck Berry, Jerry Lee Lewis. Bobby Freeman asked, "Do you wanna dance, squeeze and hug me all through the night?" and you knew she did.

I was captured. So was Paul. We followed WINS radio. Paul bought a guitar. We used my father's wire recorder, then Paul's Webcor tape machine. Holding rehearsals in our basements, we were little perfectionists. We put sound on sound (stacking two layers of our singing). With the courage to listen and cringe about how not right it was yet, we began to record.

*

We were guitar-based little rockers. Paul had the guitar. I wrote streamlined harmonies whose intervals were thirds, as I learned it from the Andrews Sisters to Don and Phil and floated it over Paul's chugging hammering-on guitar

Me and Paul and my bedroom wallpaper
in Queens, New York, 1957

technique. It was bluesy, it was rockabilly, it was
rock 'n' roll. We took "woo-bop-a-loo-chi-ba"
from Gene Vincent's "Be Bop A Lula." We stole
Buddy Holly's country flavor ("Oh Boy"), the
Everlys' harmony ("Wake Up Little Susie"). Paul
took Elvis's everything ("Mystery Train"). As
he drove the rhythm, I brought us into a vocal
blend. We were the closest of chums, making out
with our girls across the basement floor. We
showed each other our versions of masturbation

(mine used a hand). "The Girl for Me" was the first song we wrote—innocent, a pathetic "Earth Angel." In junior high we added Stu Kutcher and Angel and Ida Pellagrini.

All the while, I did a lot of homework, the shy kid's retreat. My geometry page was a model of perfection. Anything worth doing is worth doing extraordinarily well—why not best in the world?

*

My mother could prettify anything. If Darth Vader appeared in my bedroom, live at 3 a.m., and I was nine—my mother would say to him, "Dorothy, put down the mask, you're no Lancelot, then come down for mah-jongg and crumb cake." And the girls called him "Dot."

*

At twelve I was in my seventh year of being a singer when Paul and I got together. We became rehearsal freaks of fine exactitude. We did our version of doo-wop, copying Dion and the Belmonts. We wrote "A Guy Named Joe." We fused rock 'n' roll with country (rockabilly), the way Buddy Holly did. But it all took flight when Don and Phil Everly started having hits in

At a sock hop, 1958

1956. We fell out over their sound. Every syllable of every word of every line had a shine, a great Kentucky inflection, charisma in the diction. From moment to moment they worked the mic with star quality. The Everlys were our models. Paul and I wrote our songs together and practiced getting a tooled, very detailed accuracy in our harmony. We came together, with mouths, a foot apart, under a dome of very fine listening, and fashioned a sonic entity of its own.

*

I mustn't tell a soul that I'm doing this puzzle—
    a thousand pieces of Vincent van Gogh.
Looks like a sower in a flat March field,
    or an April fool at sunset.

I am with Vincent and the gorgeous madness,
    riot of beauty gone over the top—
        salmon purple, lime and brown,
    dusty rose and gold.

Under the South Pacific, I have seen the fish
    at the Barrier Reef, their sides beyond
        Matisse,
        their vibrancy more beautiful
    than anything I have seen on earth.

Except for Vincent

I want to leave this jigsaw and get on with my
        day,
    but piece by piece, I am held in awe
        by the fractured profusion,
    the jaw-dropping genius of magnificent
        dissonant
color.

So I am found in my aerie bound to the brain
    of the insane Dutchman of days gone by.
        How we suffer sensitivity.
    Stayin' in. Cast in our spells. Talent will out.
Beauty compels.

Having skipped a grade, we reached our senior year of high school about to turn sixteen. We were discouraged in our attempts to be a popular duo. At the end of the summer of '57, we met up. Paul: "Did you hear 'Hey, Doll Baby' over the summer?" I had. We groped to remember it and sketched out an entire song. By the time we heard the real Everly tune, we saw it was quite different from our sketch. Our "Hey, Doll Baby" was our own creation. We called it "Hey, Schoolgirl" and took it to Sanders recording studio on Seventh Avenue in Manhattan to make a demo for seven dollars. It was to be our last shot before we gave it up as an act. But a man named Sidney Prosen with his own small label, BIG, was in the waiting room. He bombarded us with enthusiasm when we came out. We knew the Brill Building. It was petrifying to go with the guitar on the E train from Queens and try to interest (what felt to me like) sleazy businessmen with our stuff. "Anybody looking for material here?" Rejections came after our fifteen seconds of sincere, heart-in-your-mouth auditions. "What else ya got?" It was so good that Paul and I had each other—so amazing we had the guts to cross into their world, but that was the world of the records we loved and bought. We read the record company addresses off the labels. One guy, Morty Kraft at 1650 Broadway, signed us and locked us away from all competition for six months. So we knew that trick. With Prosen we demanded the release of our record within ninety days. And he gave it to us. That fall at Bell Sound, on Thirty-fourth Street, we recorded "Hey, Schoolgirl." Paul's daddy played bass on the session. It went to #40 on the national charts, selling 150,000 copies! Suddenly we were a something in school. We had cred. We were the guys with the record on the radio. We were Tom and Jerry.

Someday I will write the "show-off book." I'll talk about doing "Hey, Schoolgirl" with Paul on Dick Clark's *American Bandstand* in Philadelphia on Thanksgiving 1957. Jerry Lee Lewis was the other guest. I see those giant stacks of fan mail lining the studio hallways. They were sent to the dancing kids, the heartthrobs. I had my own crush, watching TV after school. Now I was at the urinal, just before airtime, peeing next to one of the young stars. And then, that year, we were part of a stage revue at the Hartford State Theater, that featured LaVern Baker singing "Jim Dandy" (to the rescue). Ten acts—we were the only whites. High school cred.

*

Then in 1958 comes Betrayal. Oh so dramatic, there's hardly a play without. Is it all perception? Is it a name for unfulfilled expectation? Is it the first stone thrown or that which is perceived as such? It is a surprise blow to the gut.

Boy's love is a beautiful thing. I loved my

turned-on friend. One day, after "Hey, Schoolgirl,"
there was a phone call informing me that Tom
and Jerry was just one of the hats Paul wore
as a singer. Surprise. He was also True Taylor.
He sounded like Elvis. He was releasing a record
behind my back. Or so it felt. Perception? He's
base, I concluded in an eighth of a second, and
the friendship was shattered for life. All else is
finding forgiveness. Who have *I* hurt while in *my*
stride?

But I never forget and I never really forgive—
just collect the data and speckle the picture. Take
the blows. Call it the Inequality of Love. Eight
years later we were world-famous. You will love
your crooked neighbor with your crooked heart.

*

Think, when we talk of horses, that you see
   them
Printing their proud hoofs i' th' receiving
   earth:
For 'tis your thoughts that now must deck
   our Kings . . .

—Shakespeare (*Henry V*, Prologue)

*

Before there was Butch Cassidy and the
Sundance Kid, there was Simon and Garfunkel—
an extraordinary, a singular love affair. There is

no gay component in the two of us that I am aware of, but the way these two lives wrapped around each other is poetically stunning. From age eleven to today, a span of sixty-four years, Art and Paul have been at work to entertain, win the respect of, and dazzle one another. It worked so well that the whole world pulled up chairs to watch and listen.

Tom and Jerry, high school seniors

I can skip the smell of magnolia in the Hollywood Hills when I first came to town. But the wild aural excitement with Paul and Roy Halee, our studio engineer and coproducer, in the recording studio at Sunset and Gower stays in the story. Seven p.m. sessions would catch fire at 11. If they didn't wind down at 5 a.m., they did by 8. They were great nights. You sang a high harmony line, suspended above "All come to look for America," and then you drove the rent-a-car home from the studio, down over Santa Monica Boulevard with the rising sun behind the palms. Exceptional music glowed in your heart—I heard Simon and Garfunkel first. Other nights were about foreplay. Same hours. There was no AIDS. Paul won the writer's royalties. I got the girls. Echo made the sound wet. Glory found its way to me. Fabulous foxes, slim-hipped, B-cup, little Natalie Woods. The age of the '60s was rich America syrup, Panavision, color, a world turned on. Fellini and Michigan seem like a dream to me now, but I was aware and pleased to play my part.

*

I saw George dance with his feet in place. It's what I do in the studio control room, standing behind the engineer's board. I feel the groove and

I dance inside. George and I were in the wings at someone else's show. I was in the presence of a Beatle.

Paul and Carrie Fisher, Penny Marshall, and I were in McCartney's office. Soho Square, around '84. "My little one looks up when Linda cradles him," he says, "and sings 'Bright Eyes' to her tits."

"There's Ringo," I said to myself, never having met him before. We were both checking into the St. James's Club. He invited me up to his room.

John and Yoko, Bowie and Coco, Laurie and I returned to the Dakota after a show. Did we all win Grammys that night? John had the gift of connecting. He did it with the world, and that night with me. Sitting on the end of his bed, he called me in.

One night in London, at a noisy party, in a crowded club, George appeared behind my ear. Simon and Garfunkel had just done an outdoor concert in Wembley. I guess he had seen our show. Sweetly, intimately, he spoke of the vibe he perceived: "Your Paul is to you exactly as my Paul is to me." We play the game of "larger than life" in our business. We think it's for the fans, but even I can't get past—this disclosure from George Harrison.

To bridge the social gap in Ringo's room, the choice, in those days, was reefer or booze. Ringo was a tippler then—so endearing, so much wanting to create a palship. Aren't we in each other's magic circle of people who most understand our lives—the fame trip, the music, the money, the road, the partner's ego, the chicks, the microphone, the thrill? We danced a tipsy version of the old soft shoe, with invisible top hat and cane.

"So this is Europe," McCartney said. Wry and sly, he was poking Paul and me to get a laugh. There in his office, I posed a question to the great Beatle: "Was it always you playing keyboard on all the tunes?" "Yep," he said. I had heard that the harpsichord interlude of "In My Life" was played by George Martin, their record producer. So I pressed him with: "On *all* the tunes?"

Now John goes to work on me. Sitting next to him in his bedroom, he asks me: "Art, you just worked with Simon ["My Little Town"]. I'm being called—will I record with McCartney on his Allen Toussaint project? How was it with you two after some years apart? What should I do?" I'm to be John Lennon's adviser. Now we have social media; here you have social genius.

A highly gifted competitor, was he irked when he crossed his office to the piano? Certainly goaded, this bantam cock among his barnyard peers, Paul pounded out a white-hot "Lady Madonna" in a minute and two. He was fiercely brilliant. Never in my life have I heard the likes of that performance. Quietly he left the keyboard. "It was always me."

George took me up to the turret atop the castle he owned in Henley. We looked out on a

four-story-high papier-mâché Alp in the yard.
The space in the turret was tight. George and I
were very close. Disturbing? Thrilling?

A stranger removes your shoe and sock.
She works her thumbs between your third and
fourth toes. You open up. You bring your head
to her bosom. Her cleavage of milk and honey
surrounds your face. She opens up. It is mutual
transcendence.

I say to John: "Return to the harmony. If
you loved making the sound with him, forget
personality, forget all history, go for the jelly
roll."

Grammy night, 1975. (*Left to right*) David Bowie, Art Garfunkel,
Paul Simon, Yoko Ono, John Lennon, Roberta Flack

*

The falcon cannot hear the falconer. At the end of a four-year period of glory and gloriously hard studio work, we were tired of each other. The riffs'd been run. "Tom, get your plane right on time" has poetic heart as a song line, but the heart of the friendship was thin. We made our albums with pauses of several months, while Paul wrote the next bunch. In a pause in the winter of 1968–1969, I stepped up to career opportunity, requiring Paul's accommodation. I wasn't interested in kicking over S&G, they were extraordinary in their musical fusion, and had more albums in them. I sought a rest from him in 1970 and he couldn't abide the use I made of it—acting.

*

Secrets weary of their tyranny:
Tyrants, willing to be dethroned.

—James Joyce, *Ulysses*

SINGING IS TAKING FLIGHT. TO VIBRATE THE VOCAL CORDS, ON MIC, WITH VOLUME, AND COMMIT TO SUDDENLY "BEING THERE" IN THAT FIRST ONE-HUNDREDTH OF A SECOND OF A SYLLABLE SUNG (LIKE THE HIGH "A" AT THE END OF "AND I ONLY HAVE EYES FOR YOU") IS A LEAP OF PUBLIC COURAGE—A DIVE FROM THE LEDGE.

Paul and Artie with Roy Halee,
recording engineer and co-producer, in the control
room of Columbia's New York studio, c. 1968

Authorship may be trumpeted. It may be
declared. It may be declined.

Suddenly in my iPod, in the Southwark Station
underground, is Enrico Caruso.
He sings an aria from *The Pearl Fishers*.
Recorded at the dawn of vinyl records, it
reached me in our living room in 1946.

Heartbreaking, glorious, tenor vocal performance
    infected me when I was five.

What was it doing around the house?
Who authored the gift?

It wasn't my mother who brought the Victrola
    into our home.
Whose was the heart that cried with Caruso
    and set me on a lifelong course?
I pretend I didn't know you very well, dear Father,
    yet twenty-five years after your passing,
        here in the London tube—
            how close you are to me.
        Like the double helix of DNA, how we
        entwine.
    It was you who showed me the dive from the
ledge, the breast of the bird, the vaulting line.

Your beautiful musical soul is the author of
    mine.

*

I had an awful hard time with Paul's dad. He
made me feel misbegotten. Maybe we were unhip
suburbanites to him. (He played on Arthur
Godfrey's show.) He seemed proud to inform me
of his discovery: "Not everybody likes everybody,

and I just don't like you." I was twelve. Paul's
mother had the normal heart: love came across.
She was our grade school teacher and, like my
mother, wonderfully bright.

*

The end of S&G slipped in on me. There never
was an ending. Just "Later . . ." I started my
solo recording career with *Angel Clare,* recorded
with Roy Halee in San Francisco. At the end of
the next album, *Breakaway,* in '75, I fell deeply,
completely for Laurie Bird. Are we always
reactive, counteracting? Do we forget to return
to our own equilibrium, our moral compass first?
Did the loss of boyhood's friendship and of the
charmed circle I shared with Paul bring me to the
beautiful arms of Laurie? Why was her remoteness
good enough?
   We lived in L.A., at the Bel-Air Hotel, and
in Malibu. I discovered I liked to party. I made
Carnal Knowledge for Mike Nichols and played
alongside Jack Nicholson, to creditable reviews.
Four successful albums in the '70s, including
Watermark ('77), established me as a solo. At the
end of the decade, I was in the makeup chair,
shooting *Bad Timing* in Vienna and London for
Nic Roeg, while my #1 record "Bright Eyes" was
on the radio. I was soon to come home to the
New York City penthouse that we shared to find
Laurie had taken her life.

*

Here a silent pause to honor private pain.

*

Is it only in *my* perspective that the '60s were America's age of bust-out dynamism? Jack used to say that the failure to take the idealism—the visionary excitement of the decade—and put it into a legislative agenda turned our faith into disenchantment. Indeed, I perceived that the "money god" replaced all other values at the turn of the decade. The Beatles were over in 1970, Vietnam held us in its hopeless grip. Nixon became our leader, and young Americans, like Simon and Garfunkel, knew that the nation belonged to someone else.

*

HOPES AND DREAMS HAVE SPLIT!

Hope's with Teicher now that Ferrante's
seeing whey of Curds and Whey.
Simon's got chondroitin,
Garfunkel glucosamine—
even chlorine and sodium
after a millennium
have called a halt to salt.

*

My life, so far, is a two-act play. *Bridge Over Troubled Water* ended Act I. I arrived at a summit. The introversion of my early years tempered my nature. I was an angel singer, a homework nut; an underground man—lover of all beautiful asses, beautiful faces, beautiful bodies, boys and girls. I should have been a sculptor. So I loved James Dean and I produced a beautiful sound to express my private joy.

My brother Jules, going out with his friends, would pass me in the kitchen. I was the stay-at-home, copying the charts, in my pajamas. Al Hibbler sang "Unchained Melody," and Roy Hamilton sang the big goose-bump ballads. There

With Jack Nicholson, shooting *Carnal Knowledge*, 1971

was no such thing as *pizza* yet. English muffins were new. It was 1954.

Then came "A Rose and a Baby Ruth." I could sing "Flip, Flop and Fly" (Joe Turner) in school onstage with my new friend, Paul Simon. We had a sound so we kept practicing in my basement in Kew Gardens Hills. Upstairs at night in my bedroom, I worked at good school grades (how nerdy!) and entered Columbia College in '58. I Vespa'd across Europe in '62. I hitchhiked across America in '63, then picked up on my estranged friend, Paul, in the year of *Freewheelin'*. Dean became Dylan. We were in. The next is history. It's not this book.

What is this book? It is Act II: What follows the pinnacle? Sex on the road, just for the thrills, reading books to calm it down, the Road to walk it off, Kathryn Cermak to ease my soul, and children to end the aloneness. Singing, recording, film acting, stage entertaining, writing (hello, dear Reader), always singing, so there'll be a work life. Years roll by this way. It is my response to grand good fortune.

And this is what you think about:

*

MAJOR REVELATIONS

A) OUR ACTIONS ARE DRIVEN BY WE KNOW NOT WHAT

B) AMBITION IS MIDDLE-CLASS

C) GILLETTE COULD MAKE A BLADE
   THAT WOULD LAST A LIFETIME IF THEY
   WANTED TO
D) WE ARE NOT RESPONSIBLE FOR OUR
   FEELINGS
E) LIFE EATS LIFE
F) IT'S ALL WHERE YOU OBSERVE IT FROM
   (RELATIVITY)
G) IF ALL THINGS ARE CYCLES (NIGHT
   FOLLOWS DAY, SO DAY FOLLOWS NIGHT),
   THEN DEATH FOLLOWS LIFE, AND . . .
H) ALL IS VANITY.

*

I'll go back to my first days in Europe, to
the House of the Moroccan Students fifth
arrondissement early August 1963. Paris. Feverish
in bed. Vespa waiting in the street cast off my
soggy bedsheets enough elixir learn the bike
cobblestones drive out of town through the Bois
de Boulogne. Break there shirt change fever
passes the woods are cool. Ribbon all lyrical
two-lane road to Le Mans southwest into the
wheat fields the open field with wheat-smelling
air everywhere no helmet (first time on a
bike). Cut loose from the city from home from
pedestrian ways compelling skies perfect clouds
on Monet blue, bike at thirty-two mph, swiftest
snail. Rain at four of course wet shoes wet pants
evaporation sundown beautiful beautiful France.

Near dark I stopped at a tavern to eat. What was it in my demeanor that made the owner call out to me in the night of naïveté in a half of a century's past, in the personal pronoun: *tu as perdu ton écharpe?*

*

By the 1980s, I had sung solo on records that did well. I sustained the very painful loss of a beautiful girl. I did the Concert in Central Park with Paul in '81, then toured the world. I spent wonderful times with Penny Marshall. Then in 1983, released from touring in concert, on a BMW motorcycle, in the mountain passes of Switzerland, I began to write.

I'm in a turret of an old hotel in Scarborough. I've come to record *The Animals' Christmas* with the London Symphony Orchestra. Jimmy Webb will play piano on the session. It's his cantata and these are his notes on the musical charts taped around the cylindrical wall of this ten-foot-diameter Renaissance tower. Brass, percussion, woodwinds, strings, a window view out on the end of the strand. It's neap tide. I'm Noah. Christmastime is here. The Fair is in the past.

Since Laurie died I live in my own rarefied air. I put the "e" in "artist" every day. Monteverdi, Proust, Kubrick, I sit reclusive in the park, at the sailboat pond, near Hans Christian Andersen, and write.

I let the notebook run—December 29, 1983. Les
Arcs, ski village, France. Ineluctable modality . . .
a rower's heart, a simple water-drinking bard.
[J] *is* Stephen Dedalus and I am Leo Bloom, his
twenty-two: red and yellow ready: my forty-two
and rather "at sea." [J] has taken over, I cater
to his day. The American European. A writer's
holiday. Having read six hundred pages of *Ulysses,*
the heroes have begun to intertwine. Tomorrow
we leave on the Grande Vitesse. He is the young
marquis, he's early O'Toole, rich in frailty, he is
beautiful. He tells me he'll pull me back in the
world. I think of James Fox in *The Servant:*

> So he asks me to clean his syringe for him
>   while the medicine goes to his head;
> "Do you still have the Blistex we came with?
>   Put it on me," he said.
> I light the Ducal cigarettes
>   that pass between our silhouettes.

Paris 5ᵉ Hotel le Colbert, room 22. January 10.
The buttresses of Notre Dame are flying out my
window. [J] has been ill. His father is cutting him
off. We went to dinner at Sophie's house (Avenue
de Wagram) for eight Parisiens in their early
twenties. At 1 am they went to Le Bus Palladium
in Pigalle to dance through the night. Next day
he goes to class, Sorbonne 17ᵉ, economics post-
university level. He is being bounced. I get
caught for shoplifting underwear at Prix Unique.

We had a car accident in Luxembourg. Last night
he had a 40° fever (speck of dust). I bought him
medicine. I brought him dinner. He glistened with
sweat through the night—his bed all junked up
and cokey.

> A flock of birds was passing in the sky.
> They flew in two societies.
> I marked the leader's wings in no one's wake.

> Behind them, two cavorting stragglers fly.
> I am with them wond'ring—why don't these
> two lovers take the route the others take?

> Two lovers—or two wand'ring innocents?
> In voluntary nonparticipance,
> For joie de vol, for each the other's sake.

*

Aspen, Jack: "G, I'm your new partner. I talk.
You write it down. You can take all the credit
and the money this time." (laughing, then
pointing to the corner of his mouth, confidingly)
"Just watch this." . . . Alan's Woody Creek house
Lou Adler L.A. Lakers Jim Harrison send my
stuff to him . . . Eric and Tania's burned-out
forest in the Var turned 50 percent new green
in the first spring . . . "G (as he pushes off to
ski), on the day you die, think to yourself, 'This
is where Jack was in the third grade.'" . . . All

my life I have imagined that my life is being
viewed by a theater full of researchers. A
long watch, I hope. The experts buzz at the
poignant intermissions. The chapter endings so
slyly apt.

Captain Nately in Rome, *Catch-22*, 1970

III

From February 1979 to January 1984 I read 133
books. These 26 books stand out:

Paul Bowles, *The Sheltering Sky* (1949)
Yukio Mishima, *Spring Snow* (1968)
Richard Price, *Ladies' Man* (1978)
Jean Rhys, *Voyage in the Dark* (1934)
A. Alvarez, *The Savage God* (1971)
Marcel Proust, *À la recherche du temps perdu,*
     Book 2 (1925)
Jean Dorst, *The Life of Birds*, Vol. 1 (1971)
Edward Gibbon, *The Decline and Fall of the
     Roman Empire* (1787)
J. D. Salinger, "The Inverted Forest,"
     Uncollected Short Stories (1947)
Gary Zukav, *The Dancing Wu Li Masters*
     (1979)
David Hume, *An Enquiry Concerning Human
     Understanding* (1748)
J. P. Donleavy, *The Destinies of Darcy Dancer,
     Gentleman* (1977)
Gompert, Mandelbaum, Garwin, Barton, *Nuclear
     Weapons and World Politics* (1977)
Virginia Woolf, *A Room of One's Own* (1929)
Saint Augustine, *Confessions* (AD 398)

Martin Buber, *On Judaism* (1909–51)
William James, *The Varieties of Religious Experience* (1902)
Thornton Wilder, *The Bridge of San Luis Rey* (1927)
Emil Ludwig, *Napoleon* (1926)
Vladimir Nabokov, *Lectures on Literature* (1980)
Miguel de Cervantes, *Don Quixote* (1604)
W. Somerset Maugham, *The Razor's Edge* (1944)
Peter Gay, *The Enlightenment: The Rise of Modern Paganism* (1966)
Michel de Montaigne, *Travel Journal* (1580)
Johan Huizinga, *The Waning of the Middle Ages* (1919)
James Joyce, *Ulysses* (1921)

*

When I was fourteen I lay down with you,
   our eyes misty with urge,
      our mouths in open moan

The sun was big in those late afternoons
   swollen and red-ripe,
      it filtered in stripes on wallpaper
   and wet linen.

   —Do you know what we are?
you said

*

(Left to right) Mike Nichols, Candice Bergen,
Art Garfunkel, Jack Nicholson

Baby come back. Any kind of fool could see
there was something in everything about you.
February 8, 1984. I live alone in the bee-
loud glade. My heart breaks daily for Laurie
Bird. . . . Necromancing. I have begun to read the
dictionary. Z to A. Why not? Collected pretty
shells, shaded meanings—vernier, vermilion, venal,
veery . . . How much is too much turning around
to look at the people you pass? My brothers and
Penny. Cortina d'Ampezzo, we weave our tracks
in a snowy braid. . . . It is not given to man to
know his needs.

*

Jack and I in Bloomingdale's. We buy four pairs of moving gloves. He says they're for when you're on the move. Adding my name to the hotel's book of famous people, I scan through the forms of politeness on the pages preceding mine: wordy Spielberg, formal Streisand, gracious Michael Jagger.

*

Rolling Stone cover, October 11, 1973

THEN ONE DAY I LACED UP MY NEW BALANCE
SNEAKERS, LEFT MY KITCHEN, AND WALKED ACROSS
CENTRAL PARK, TO MY OLD ALMA MATER, TO
THE GEORGE WASHINGTON BRIDGE. I CARRIED
NEXT TO NOTHING, JUST A PAPERBACK, MAPS, AND
SOME UNDERWEAR. FORT LEE FOR LUNCH, DOWN
TO SECAUCUS, RISING THROUGH WEST ORANGE.
I CROSSED NEW JERSEY IN SEVEN DAYS, SINGING
WITH MY EARPHONES, WRITING IN MY NOTEBOOK.
I WAS JOHNNY APPLESEED, WALT WHITMAN, AFTER
THE PINNACLE, FIFTY-THREE PACES A MINUTE,
SEVENTEEN MILES A DAY, FORTY EXCURSIONS,
I REACHED THE PACIFIC.

Do or deign. Marvin Gaye was shot today.
I follow the Mason-Dixon line to Gettysburg.
March 31, 1984. Wrightsville, Pa. Thirty-five miles
along the Susquehanna. . . . I'd like to know
the age of a tree, and in its species' expected
duration of life, compute where it stands in its
maturity. I might be walking among my peers.

In size places, a windbreak of schoolgirls
play sway in a Maryland meadow.

*

Largent, West Virginia. JUNE 15. Walking America,
night setting in, no cars, no phone, in pain.
Necessity invents. We knock on the door of the
house up the hill, and we're kindly taken in.

Three twentyish girls playing cards. Rock 'n' roll
came from their window. The girls were hippies
on welfare. We had two pairs of legs in jeans.
It was Friday night, and they were in mid-trip
on acid. They taught me about the under-the-
radar population in America—no registering for
anything, no taxes. They recognized me but found
their disbelief wrestling with a miracle. What are
you doing *here?* Go explain that truth is stranger.

*

Can I look through whatever is today
and see what once was Proust's Cambrai?

*

"Wherever you go, you're always there."

This is said to spoil the spell
     of being "taken" by a place.

When I was a boy of seven or so
     daytime radio would take me to
     pictures of Western America.

Before there was Paul Harvey,
     there was Arthur Godfrey
     and Our Gal Sunday.

Listening to the national radio,
     I felt connected to Montana.
     Americana got a hold on me.

I am watching the beautiful light-
    fall here at the end of the day
    in southern Minnesota. Iowa's only
    a few miles away.

Have I not entered the mental tableau
    that radio created for me
    sixty years ago? Am I not within
    the pixels of the picture here today?

And am I, at last a noble and titled
    Englishman, taken by the sky
    or by my own blue eye?

*

Captain Conti shoots the shit with me on the
pilot's deck, the bridge. It's Friday the 13th
of July, ten at night. The tugboats have taken
us into the reflection of the full moon on the
Mississippi. My inner life is set again in motion.
    —Shippers are crying the blues, he says,
exports are way down. America's heyday is over.
    We sail under the Greater New Orleans Bridge.
He has promised the World's Fair a blast of the
horn and he leaves me, reborn by the rail, as we
glide past the fair—darkly, sage. Fireworks cover
and christen the eye for the soon-to-be-visible
stars in the sky.
    So much brilliant daylight is a challenge to
the eye. So I start off with coffee up in the
wheelhouse. The captain tells me he's looking

for A. A. Brill's translation of Freud's *The Interpretation of Dreams*. It gives him the giggles to read stuff like "Misers tend to be constipated." His quarters are below mine, so now I must watch my ass.

We are sailing to Galveston, threading through oil rigs.

—They have just invented a directional drill that can reach, at an angle, for miles undersea. So now they can steal oil from the neighboring wells.

Looking sternward, rotating counterclockwise in Galveston harbor, a pilot's boat shoots clockwise into view. Container-loaded and spring-loaded I am at last ready to take a ship. Gulls in a vortex take the eye above the pilot's boat . . . to the west, to a bay, and to mainland USA—Oil City, Texas, seven miles away. Now aimed at the Atlantic, valediction complete, we climb onto a sheet of iridescence . . . beautiful, limitlessness . . .

*

I walk the ship from end to end, watching it part the waves. A part of loving is knowing . . . water excited, diaphanous folds. . . . I have come to know, somewhat, the sight of the beautiful foam below. Now the Courtship continues to sail amid marble. I look for my love to grow. . . . and we're gone.

*

We sailed for a while at six degrees
almost north up the Florida coast.
At ten after midnight, I turned in my bed
        and felt our direction shift.
"This must be the start of the crossing,"
I mused, with my ear to the mattress,
        engrossed in the rocky motion
        of solid time getting longer
                the deeper we drift.

*

ALMOST ACROSS THE ATLANTIC, THE FREIGHTER
CARRIES THE MOURNER.

I catch myself in close-up looking into
    three concentric rings.

If they combed the world to find me,
    covered all my stomping grounds on land
    and raked the sea—
    only at longitude seventeen west
    and latitude forty-eight north,
    four hundred miles from the Brittany coast
    in the hull of a night-riding voyager,
    loitering in the pantry.
    Spooning pear juice from a tin,
    remembering her love for pears,
    and staring at rings in a tin sea,
    would they find me.

*

MOTORCYCLING IN EUROPE

Not unlike Rimbaud, I tend to go my own
invented way, beyond fame. I live in soliloquy, and
I don't mind the wolf in me nor all the rugged
barren beauty round my shoulders as I ride alone.

It is the eve of September 1984, August 31,
that clearest cusp of the calendar. Autumn has
begun in the Hebrides. The day has come to the
end.

Nineteen hundred and eighty-four kilometers
of two-lane blacktop have passed from the
Faubourg du St. Honoré, through the Bois de
Boulogne, La Porte de St. Cloud, Argenteuil,
up the Seine, Vétheuil. Rouen 'n' onward
west—across Normandie, always in sunshine—
Repentigny—kick into fifth to the ferry at St.
Malo then the Anglo-Saxon section commences:
Southampton to Soho Square—I interrupt to go
to London on a train, to the art department
at CBS, to Intourist (London to Leningrad)—to
the bike and the south and the centerline, past
Stonehenge, through the Cotswolds, to Leeds, we
weave around the spine of England's Midlands to
Northumberland in summer wind and over the
border to Scotland . . . there's no one in this
country, pathetic little road, purple mountains,
heather and brown, follow me down the motorway
to Glasgow, town of Scrooge and Marley buildings
built around the '80s, empty since the '60s,
downtown Stonehenge, train station space that

great place I sit in the sunlit morning among
men who don't work, with the Firth beside . . .
birds gossip in the gleaming of the Clyde . . .
and I am reading Edmund Wilson, listing north-
northwest, and dreaming beyond Lochs Lomond
and Ness, over glenned loveliness to the serious
beauty of the Highlands. The clouds and I are
attracted and held in thrall. It rains. Fall weather
emerges at Invergarry, and in reply we ride to
the Atlantic on a ferry from the mainland to the
Isle of Skye. Keen the air, I clean in the rain in a
Portree laundromat. Today, herring gulls, ferry to
the Hebrides, land in the minority. Uig to Tarbert,
across the little Minch. As Skye fades into water,
its final fields in silhouette climb north-northwest
to cliffy falls.

And I have come to Stornoway, 1984, away
from Paris. Across the Isle of Lewis, and from its
leeward side, I ride alone to the sea at last. Under
a shelf of risen rain, the northwest sun emerges
and slips slowly on its way to set. Chastened
and enchanted and forgiven again, a silhouette is
slowly rising into it.

Laurie Bird

IV

We both had cotton T-shirts from
   Redfish Lake in Idaho,
   mine green, hers white.
We had had them from before we met.
At night in our bliss, she slept in only this,
   the captured sailfish nestled across
   her perfect chest.

In the morning at the dawn of consciousness,
   I would nuzzle under her armpit
   where the blond hair was.
There, in her smell, was my elemental
   resting place, straddler of dreams
   and the day,
I see that cotton short sleeve
   cut her beautiful bicep at the top.
Under it within that crumpled skinny harbor,
   safe again in love's conviction,
   I long to return.

*

Overdubbing.

Into the heart of Nashville this morning I brought Tolstoy—*Confession* (1879). Under speckled autumn light, before the capitol steps, I retraced with Leo his search for faith—how urbanity, rationality, and the life of wealth were obstacles in the pursuit.

Yesterday, Amy Grant sang on our album. From out of church music she arrives at the date addressing the singer's challenge at the microphone—to offer the inner self.

And where is my faith? Has there not been for me a loss in the meaning of everything since the day she died?

Tolstoy toiled with the common man, an attempt to be God's instrument. Amy came with a student's air. And I employ these people to come and put their feeling in the tape.

It has become a Gothic cathedral to me, this *Animals' Christmas*—an anachronism. Jimmy and I are stonecutters, building a structure in praise of God.

*

Let toin be toinbee
and let all toins be.

The span of an octave,
a handful of books,
the stretch from pinky to thumb,
I grab five books

with an eight-note grip—
six inches of literature,
two to three months,
the size of a hen,
a season of reasoning,
cut lit for feed,
I read for greed.

*

syrinx (sir´ ingks) n.	The song organ in birds; a panpipe *Syrinx*. In Greek mythology, a nymph pursued by Pan and changed into a reed, from which Pan made his pipes.
syntony (sin´ tə-nē) n.	The harmonizing or tuning of transmitters and receivers each to the other; resonance.
syncline (sing´ klīn) n.	The axis of a fold from which rock strata incline (Is it the pinnacle?)
supertonic (sü-pur ton´ ik) n.	The second tone of a scale (Is it the ??)
supernal (sü-pur´ nəl) adj.	Heavenly
stover (stō´ vər) n.	A coarse roughage used as feed for livestock
stager (stā´ jər) n.	A person of experience in some profession, way of life, etc.
specular (spek´ yə-lor) adj.	Pertaining to a mirror

specious (spē′ shəs) adj.	Apparently good or right though lacking real merit; superficially pleasing
solipsism (sol′ ip-siz-əm) n.	The theory that only the self exists, or can be proven to exist
simony (sī′ mə-nē, sim′ ə) n.	The making of profit out of sacred things
sidereal (sī-dēr′ ē-əl) adj.	Determined by or from the stars
servitor (sûr′ vi-tər) n.	One who is in the service of another; attendant
senescent (sə-nes′ ənt) adj.	Growing old; aging
sempre (sem′ prā) adv.	[musical directions] Throughout
sciamachy (sī-am′ ə-kē) n.	Act or instance of fighting a shadow or an imaginary enemy
sawyer (sô′ yər) n.	One who saws, esp. as an occupation
satyriasis (sā′ tə-rī′ ə-sis) n.	Abnormal, uncontrollable sexual desire in men

*

When I was twenty, I was crazy inside. It was 1961—a year of extremism, of personal greatness. In the depth of my being I was bound for glory. On the surface, I didn't know what to do. I went for becoming an architect. I liked their gum-bottom

shoes. I had little success in bedding the girls—
they mostly represented failure. My family, my
home was a source of comfort. Sanford Greenberg
was my gold standard. Each morning I communed
with God. I was small, but I was chosen.

*

I HAVE A FRIENDSHIP MADE OF GOLD WITH
SANFORD G. HE IS MY DEAREST. WE ROOMED
TOGETHER IN THE EARLY '60S, AT COLUMBIA
COLLEGE. WE REMAINED SOLIDLY BOUND IN OUR
MUTUAL LOVE OF LIFE, OF CHARACTER, AND OF
EACH OTHER.

This is our town, this friendship of ours.
We are the ones who can't look at everything
        hard enough.
Let us go back to the day
    of the fiftieth year you were my mate.
It was early December, two thousand eight,
    fifty years since fifty-eight.

What is it all but luminous?
Tears blur the vision, sweet indecision
    to be or to curl up back in the womb.
We had our room, four-o-six,
    your hair was more shiny brown.
Who knew from Nixon and student protest?
Toads like me, through a deprivation of
        stimuli,
    let in the aroma of autumn turning winter

on the campus as if it were Art in New
    York.
Breughel-touched. . . . *tefillin* by the
    window,
Ivy League Christmas Kingsmen Yule Log
eggnog fire glow. And after glow?

Do any of us ever realize life while we have it,
    eyes wet and radiant and with a
        shehecheyanu?
     Yes we do.

*

love moves everything
(why else do I sing?)
all it touches is thus moved

*

Three days of singing in Montserrat have passed.
Eighty percent of my work has been done.
Under a butternut tree,
   Ralph Vaughan Williams is playing.

I am a plumb bar swaying,
   yielding to the inclination of the wind.

Free to rotate, out on a limb,
   in a hammock shaped like a sideways "J,"
   and hung from a single cord,

I lean toward autobiography.

When the wind decides,
    it blows through the Theme by Thomas Tallis
    at the base of the tree,
    and changes the stereo on me.

                     *

Having recorded *Angel Clare, Breakaway,
Watermark, Fate for Breakfast, Scissors Cut* in
the '70s, I am in the British West Indies
producing *The Animals' Christmas* with Geoff
Emerick at AIR Studios. Chartres cathedral is
my metaphor.

    Now the side walls are going up.
    Piano, harp, and vibraphone, in repeating
        arpeggios,
      are as masonry—a field of articulated lines.
    Apertures left for a trumpet decree, a cor
        anglais.
    Strings and woodwinds finish the stone.
    Through the clerestory, children's voices
      descend upon David's City.
    Around the base, a donkey motif
      like a tom-tom frieze in low relief.
    Stained-glass windows, angel-drawn, arrive at
        the site.
    Echo and I are the colored light.

*

Past striving, I continue to kick around.
   I've had career. I've been in love.
   Why persist?
Another "digital delinquency" has stopped the
      mix
   for almost a week.
Buttresses, stepped and stone-finished,
   lie on the ground about to fly.
I hang with the masons while I think about
      my life
   . . . my father . . . Children!
   To complete my life?
   To give the trip as a gift?
   To not be the end to the branch
    of the tree of genes?
   What does it mean?

I fought with my father just last week
   and could have pulled the whole house down,
   ripped the charade of family apart,
   tired of being misunderstood.
But I called him later and patched it up.
Just why did I call?
   For one of the Ten Commandments?
   For: Do unto others as you *will* have others
      do unto you?
Or was it the genes we share?
Could it be that the way we wonder is more
      alike
   than anyone else we know?

*

On August 17, 1986, my father died. Jacob Israel, traveling salesman, ardentest heart of all.

Grand Central Station. Monarch Manufacturing.
Leather bomber jackets on a road trip . . .
Yonkers. June verdure. Train cadence. Morning
at ten . . . Monday. The Hudson. To my brother
Jerry. Green Palisades. Four long homers away.
Twenty-five-story-high purple and brown stone
cliffs . . . brownstone. The East Sixties . . .

Michelangelo's *Pietà*

The Tappan Zee. My brother will come from
Woodstock to Rhinecliff to meet me.

All hail Henry Hudson's "discovery," and how
nobody knew it before. Beauty increases above
the bridge as it widens . . . Croton-Harmon,
FDR. Billie. Glenn Miller. My father's fedora.
Bogie. Gable. Peck. There in his car, samples in
back, adoring his kids in his mind. And leaving us
behind. To drive beside the Bear Mountain Bridge.
In '45, with his third son born, his bliss must
have known no bounds. Manhood's decree. His
legitimacy.

Haul those sample cases. The strapped black
plastic three-by-two lead valise. (Any bottles
inside?) The river perceptibly narrows to
five hundred feet across . . . then bridge—
Poughkeepsie, a big name in my father's life.
Who was the buyer? Where was the hotel?
Was there a girlfriend? . . . Was there another
life? . . . Poughkeepsie. The war won. Great days
for Brooklyn. Durocher, still a bum. It wasn't
just Furillo. It was Cox and Pafko and Gene
Hermanski. And light *was* more golden then and
hopeful, so fewer pollutants were in the air. We
was robbed. . . . The American way of letting
money have its say . . . any way.

*

I think, therefore I am.
I feel, therefore I love.

I yearn to tell my all,
* my everyone, to believe.*
Therefore I come to San Gimignano
* in the late afternoon on Christmas Eve.*

Believe in the heart's insistence
* to rule throughout existence.*
Believe in the Buddha, Muhammad
* and Moses and in Christian prayer.*
Your faith, like that of the mason
* of a hill town in the darkening*
* Middle Age air—put it there.*

Kathryn Ward Cermak, c. 1987

V

When I'm away for a while I come home and see
the obvious—those drapes need cleaning, this room
is too dark, I'm lonely. Back from Montserrat in
autumn '85, I open my months of mail. There, a
picture of actress Kathryn Luce, my future bride.
Just back home alone and horny, I go to the
phone.

*

I wanna be like Jesus, draped across his
    mother's lap
Michelangelo's masterpiece, the marble *Pietà*
A figure of adoration to nuns, mothers, and
    lonely hearts
Slim-hipped idol in a loincloth, sculpted body
    parts.
The thrust of the trochanter, the Virgin
    Mary's pride
Stone's holy answer, with erotic thrill denied.

Hang me on the X's, with Marley's martyred
    fame
And a skinny superhero's frame.

*

A: I'm afraid of you.
K: You should be.
A: You're a power.
K: It's your karma to get me.
A: You're the other half of my disease.
K: What's that?
A: The cure.

*

Things are a little bit different—now when I go
to the laundry basket, a pair of young woman's
underwear is in my whites. Deeper down, beyond
other late nights, I come upon another girl's
underwear.

*

So he always needed to fill up a room.
He acted big—a kind of play.
And I found it easy to give him his space,
    to ramble his way . . . and that's all okay.

Then he earned the spotlight—he was funny
    he was right, he was never uptight
    when I was around.

I was a "BOUNCE," a sort of wall
    and he of course had the ball.

*

So I'm having a dinner with Paul last night, just the two of us, at his favorite restaurant in the Broadway theater area. I make a statement of fact about something. He quietly interjects, "Or so you claim." He is amused by his own slightly competitive comment, and he tells me the recent story of his fondness for the phrase: He was in a taxi in Chicago. The driver pointed out the Sears Tower proudly as the tallest structure in the U.S. So Paul said, with a knowing tone, "Well, I don't think it's taller than the Empire State Building." Driver: "Yes it really is." Paul (quietly): "I don't think so." Driver: "No, the Sears *is* the tallest." Paul (very quietly now): "Or so you claim." Paul laughs—New York won't be bested by Chicago.

Now Paul goes on to a new subject with, "Did I tell you this—you'll be amused . . ." I cut him off with, "Let me be the judge of that." I laugh at the obvious tease (parallelism). He says, a bit more soberly, "Okay, you'll make the call." He is not amused.

*

WALKING AMERICA

Davenport. The third of May. Six p.m. Minutes from the Mississippi. I stalk the epiphany. Spring waxes in apple-green trees, in this Hall of Fame of American streets. Two little boys "hello" at me. I point to the rising moon . . . faint and full.

I too get weary and sick of tryin' . . . six feet
from The River at high noon. I took a room at
the Hotel Mississippi, downtown Davenport, and
ate a pizza while the Lakers played Portland in
the playoffs . . . fifteen hundred and forty-eight
full moons ago Huck was rafting here. (And so
were you and I.) (Or was Huck with Jim that
night, have I recast a sentimental Twain?)

*

Good pitch is simple honesty.
Correcting pitch with PRO TOOLS
	is a simulated way.
All of our days, the searching needs
	for unalloyed truth and beauty lead.

Morality played to win is a
	plate of tin.

*

I tried to write a poem to Kim
	but her image mesmerized my mind.
Her blondness made me blind.
So I calmly sought to find the subtle
	honest feelings that I have for her inside

. . . I don't get her. What is she?
Lemon meringue?
She's a hellcat. Is that what I need?

Kathryn and Arthur (Kim and Artie), c 1986

Her identity lies in her loves.
The love of man and woman as one
   is first of all with her . . . m m m

*

How many books of the writers I read:

9 Balzac
8 Tolstoy, Dickens, Proust

7 Twain, Henry James
6 Flaubert, Rousseau, Plato, Rhys
5 Hardy, Dostoevsky, Freud, Joyce, Austen
4 Eliot, Nabokov, Goethe, Woolf, Salinger,
  Barzun, Roth, Gay, McEvedy
3 Thackeray, Chekhov, Wilder, Defoe, Kissinger,
  Mann, Faulkner, Hemingway, Voltaire, Jung,
  A. J. P. Taylor, Fielding, Wharton, Kant,
  Trollope, Mead, Butler, Bellow, Ikeda,
  Ouspensky, Fisher, Mailer, Wodehouse,
  Heidegger, Tom Wolfe, Graves

*

I was born to fuck the girls of the
    Junior League.
I know they're Wellesley women
    now with equestrian intrigue.
But they want their daddy's
    spanking one more time.

A fox in her underwear's worth
    the hunt.
To part the pearls and penetrate
    that neoclassic front
And play the only jazz on the
    upper east side.

*

We are what we eat, not the things of words
We're made of the meat of the wings of birds

What's It Like to Be a Film Actor?

I made *Carnal Knowledge* for Mike Nichols in
'71 and *Bad Timing* for Nicolas Roeg at the
end of the '70s as Laurie died. With the first
we worked mostly in Vancouver. A driver would
bring Nicholson and me to the set in the morning.
There, in the backseat, Jack and I would run
lines, then sing "Fire and Rain" to be in harmony
as performers. I played the innocent. In *Bad
Timing*, shot mostly in Vienna, Harvey Keitel was
investigating why my lover, Theresa Russell, had
tried to take her life (but did not succeed, while
Laurie in New York succeeded with doing just
that). I was Alex Linden, working at NATO, a man
of mystery. At the end of a day's shoot, Jack and
I stood on the deck in the fine mist, naked outside
the pool, into the Canadian sunset. We played
a lot of Cat Stevens. But in London, with *Bad
Timing*, the day ended with the learning of the
next two, three, or four pages of the script in
the bathtub atop the Portobello Hotel. Theresa was
across the hall having an affair with the director.
I was intense—memorization, all the different spins
that could be put into the lines. Psychoanalysis.

*

Suppose they served horsemeat when we
    ordered Big Macs
And for every shepherd's pie they baked a
    dog.

What we won't eat is our wont and our
    custom;
What we consume is our trust.

Thus the London restaurant chain of
    GARFUNKELS

*

I drifted north on the first day off to look at
    the Londoners,
    air up the ailerons, track the topography,
      feel England
    rise from the Thames. Marylebone Station,
      Wellington Road,
    noon at the ridge of North End Way. . . .

A particular type of Romantic will praise
    the Hampstead Heath—
    those who love the upland view, those few
      of you with eyes
    that roam over the St. Paul dome to
      Byzantium.

I carry on down the northern slope.
View is lost, all guiding signs are gone, but
    one—
    high above the heath, beneath a cloudy day,
      two lines askew
    converge for you in skywriting. What does
      it mean?
    The Byzantine beyond the Adriatic art?

O poor heart. You are lost. Earth eludes.
You are left with skyward moorings.

*

Does anyone notice the faint aroma of slowly
decaying flesh? I'm depressed. All is vanity.
Where is meaning? We are eating and excreting
organisms. We're led by maître d's. We rest our
Western Civilization on plumbing . . . the plumbers
are here behind me in the kitchen. "A nipple broke
off," the super says of the pipes above the soffit.
Six recessed lights have become showerheads. I am
weeping within for want of procreation. Suddenly
the first snow falls. Like *The Animals' Christmas*
cover, spotted in white, fat flakes are filling the
window. Why does the national deficit haunt
me? We live on borrowed time. Why does all the
dumbness hurt me? . . . I piss. The plumbing's
turned off. I leave it. I am trying to mix music
and commerce and it's killing me. I feel the failure
of proper promotion of *The Animals' Christmas*
and now that it is the eleventh of December,
I conclude I'm not wanted that much by The
Company. . . .
But I make this new album I privately cherish,
and now I must sing through it all—through the
death of Jacob Israel, the loss of Laurie Bird,
the TV ad for *Graceland*, the perfect Christmas
gift, the triumph of politics I ain't got, through
baldness and bad brotherhood, thousands of
librettos left out at the factory, streams coming

down in the kitchen behind me through pipes
I share with Mr. Tisch below. I go to sing the
purple plum, the midnight blue, the forest green.

*

AFTER CHERNOBYL I WATCHED US ALL SLIP INTO THE ACCEPTANCE OF A NUCLEAR-TAINTED WORLD. MAY 1986.

Ames in the afternoon. The worst of all
possible nuclear catastrophes has happened. I drive
across Iowa, heading for Omaha, keeping an eye

With my mother in Israel, c. 1983

With my father in Israel, c. 1983

on the northwest sky. It's a small world after all.
Radioactivity is all a hype now only ZZ Top can
groove.

*

I killed a bird at Altamont, just at the start of
The Lark Ascending—southeast Kansas. It never
figured the wind to be so strong. It struggled
across my hellish aisle and failed SMACK into my
windshield, above the radio dial. It rolled, stunned
or killed, on the blacktop. Down from sixty-five, I
backed up to have a look.

A bird friend was there in attendance. It
stood in the other lane, keeping its distance . . .

violas enter from the slain bird as she lay on her side . . . then I was alone with her, slayer and prayer, pray-er and prey . . . I coulda been Dean under credits in *Rebel Without a Cause*. Going down with Darwin, I touched her gossamer wing.

*

WHITHER THE PEOPLE WHO ARE MOVED AWAY WHEN A SCHOOL EXPANDS?

Mostly it's sports that drove those old families out. Arenas of epic proportions. (I'll be playing them.) Alumni donations. Limping students. . . . Under a tent off the side of the ballpark (Huskers—Oklahoma in the top of the first) beneath concrete bleachers, rows A to triple Z for the football games, are fifteen masseurs. The U. of N. track lies near in the noon sun. Trucks for the ETV Network are here ("E" for education). Under a hundred fifty fingers practiced in dislocations, the track and field boys lie in wait.

*

On leave from the army at Annecy, the
    young Frenchman
  boards the train at Aix-les-Bains.
He enters the compartment where I sit alone
    with the poems of James Joyce.
My *Flowers of Evil*, Baudelaire, sits on the
    chair between us.

He is going home to Marseille,
  with the conquering air of the "distingué."
His way becomes my route.

The importance of blue jeans when they're
      medium blue,
    slightly big, and a little puckered from
    starch.
(VALENCE) He wears a black leather jacket
      over a black-and-white-
    checked flannel shirt. I read the *Ballad of
    a Soldier*,
    Alyosha, on his lips compelling empathy like
      Julien Sorel.
He is adorable.

Now he stands to stow his bag on the shelf
      above
    across from us. . . .
Why wouldn't the Lord love me
    even as I am transfixed by his ass?
Ask me to tie his shoe now as a game—
    and give all my love in a swoon of shame.

Most of all I'm nonplussed by where my heart
has taken me. Headless author, I see myself
embarrassed and askance.
    But hear the heart's information. Wear your
choices affectionately. Make it embraceable, dance
in the vastness of your own inner grace.

August 4, 2009. Soon I will come to Hoisington, deep in the heart of Kansas in August under the sun beautiful air not yet noon. If this rectangle state were an envelope, then I paid the postage, I've come to where you address the name. . . . I am *accompli*, I've been to sea. Now rolling bands of plains accompany me. The broad sweep, violas play with bows long drawn with celli maroon in harmony.

Sweet land of liberty, I stand amid—I am Whitman's kid. I am Prometheus bound to be bicoastal. From spring to remains I sing in my chains. . . . I am Avi Garman-Singer, Avraham to some, my father Jacob Israel sold garments. (He broke his back upon it, but that's a Willy Loman sonnet.)

I have come to address this letter: Mr. and Mrs. . . . Challenged-by-Identity, you, me, America. We're all at a loss by the nouns. It's in the verbs that we see ourselves—drivin', takin' it, reckoning, assembling the cast of man, outlasting.

Primeval Kathryn and Arthur

VI

Wintertime nighs. Perhaps I'll light a fire this year. Maybe I'll put away her things.

*

Kathryn Ward Cermak found Minneapolis too stultifying for an actress. She came to New York City with a chip on her shoulder and soon found herself doing book covers for Anthony Loew, the same photographer I did my *Scissors Cut* album cover with. Tony was a straight shooter. I believed him when he put her 8x10 glossy in the mail. "Here's an amazing girl I recently worked with . . ." Love slipped in on me. It was organic. It wasn't the thing I thought I was looking for, but it felt so good. This was something else again.

In the late '80s, I put a band together and started to gig. I began to read the Random House dictionary and started to walk across the USA. I put out a book, *Still Water,* and walked my baby down the aisle.

*

It's the organza that's got her.
That's why this is happening.
A sea of billowy white stuff
    must enfold her limbs.

No one said "Kathryn"
    before "clothed in crinoline,"
but the ears that hear cathedral
    bells are Kim's.

And they're dripping, tripping down
    for her, who'll walk no more
        on fields unfrosted;
What a dream—
    what hypoglycemian hymns.

But shouldn't we make her happy?
Mustn't her heart be glad?
Are we not bound to ride her train
    of sequins and darts
        and all the pictures our hearts
        have had?

*

From February 1984 to January 1989 I read 198
books. These 26 books stand out:

Thomas Mann, *The Confessions of Felix Krull,
    Confidence Man* (1955)
L. N. Tolstoy, *What Is Art?* (1896)

Wedding Day, September 18, 1988

Iris Murdoch, *A Severed Head* (1961)
William Thackeray, *Vanity Fair* (1847)
Thornton Wilder, *The Ides of March* (1948)
Constantin Stanislavski, *An Actor Prepares* (1936)
Lucretius, *On the Nature of the Universe*
   (c. 54 BC)
Frances FitzGerald, *Fire in the Lake* (1972)
Lao Tsu, *Tao Te Ching* (6th century BC)
Richard Ellmann, *James Joyce* (1959)
Herodotus, *The Histories* (446 BC)

Edith Wharton, *The House of Mirth* (1905)
Julian Jaynes, *The Origin of Consciousness in the Breakdown of the Bicameral Mind* (1976)
Vladimir Nabokov, *The Enchanter* (1939)
Harold Schonberg, *The Lives of the Great Composers* (1970)
Thomas Hobbes, *Leviathan* (1651)
Carrie Fisher, *Postcards from the Edge* (1987)
Michel Montaigne, *Essays* (1580)
Sigmund Freud, *The Ego and the Id* (1923)
Friedrich Nietzsche, *A Nietzsche Reader* (1880s)
Mark Twain, *Life on the Mississippi* (1882)
Fyodor Dostoevsky, *Notes from Underground* (1849)
George Eliot, *Middlemarch* (1872)
Francis Parkman, *The Oregon Trail* (1849)
Confucius, *The Analects* (c. 500 BC)
Charles Dickens, *Bleak House* (1853)

*

Egyptian limo driver, Thirty-eighth and Mad,
    steamer and shiatsu on the mezzanine;
Joseph and his brothers—does it mean
    estrangement, wasn't he scorned for his
    virtue first, thrown with a coat in a pit?
Is it his wits with which he fights, hitchhiking
    with the Ishmaelites to Cairo, to a jail cell,
    and eventually to the Pharaoh
    via Dream Interpretation?
    "lean cows eat up fat cows"

Didn't he sit like this and miss his father
 and baby Ben, and turn again to the
  riddle—
 "Let seven lean cows equal seven tough
  years?"
 (say Seventy-nine to Eighty-six)

He didn't expect enthronement or the
 fortune-telling royalties; he didn't exactly
 say, "Buy cheap, sell dear."
But there he sits, the Pharaoh's prize,
 trade minister of grain supplies, disguised
 as planned, when his brothers appear

It isn't easy being the fortunate son, the
middle of three brothers—
 There's skin-colored wood in the sauna, and
three Caucasians blending in. I, on my orange
towel, in the corner (next to the rust-colored
sand in the timer) stare at fire in the rock bin.

*

Take me to the tannery.
Into the closet of cobra and crocodile.
Let me linger a while with skin,
 stacked and slaughtered. Take me in.

Let me hide when the tanners begin the
 dyeing process.
Close my nose but let me watch the washing.

Stain the beast in original sin.
Put his open mouth before me,
   let me take it on the chin,
   and whisper past rows of pointy teeth within
   the ghastly masquerader:
   "See you later . . ."

*

A line is descending from infinite space.
 The life of a man. A geometric curve.
 Intuitive fire in the infant's face—
  the heavenly place of childhood.
   Hang-gliding down to the twenties,
   a man comes of age hovering
     over rapture and ravine,
       he touches earth at twenty-three,
       still captured by the wind,
         and buoyed—he runs among
         us here. Engaged.
           A down-to-earth man
            in his gait,
             28.

*

SEPTEMBER 18, 1988—WE PLIGHTED OUR TROTH,
STOOD ON THE BOARDS, SWORE BEFORE ALL OF
OUR FRIENDS: "THIS IS MY BELOVED." SUCH PROMISE
SEEMED TO FRUCTIFY AND INDUCED EMOTIONAL
SECURITY THEREBY. SO YOU MOVED IN.

I am Mr. Mickey Mouse and she's my Minnie
  Mouse.
Around the house she's Mighty Mouse.
O mounted spouse divine,
O scintillant Mouse be mine.
Be mighty, be mini, or any amount of chantilly.
Be winged Minty Mouse, timeless and sublime.

X

NOW THAT I AM A TOURING CONCERT ARTIST,
HERE IS MY TRIBUTE TO JAMES TAYLOR.

I sing to James Taylor before every show I
do. I warm up in my dressing room to "Handy
Man," "Sarah Maria," "Song for You Far Away,"
"Sweet Baby James," "Copperline," and about
twenty other favorites. Then I go from James's
bass-baritone to tenor singing with the Everly
Brothers—first Don, later Phil.

While I'm unisoning with James, my reverence
rises, my heart and mind become engaged in the
sober intelligence of the song and the beauty
of the singing. James's accuracy of pitch is like
a trader's honesty. To me, it has always been
paramount in singing. There is an illuminating love
of living things—all of them here on earth—that
lies within the tenderness of his line readings
(listen to his song "Gaia" from *Hourglass*). If vocal
cord vibration were like surfing off the swelling
of the heart, James would be my favorite rider

on the cusp—a little in the air, sublime in the spray.

It's no accident that the Beatles' newly formed Apple Records signed James Taylor at its inception. He is the finest of us Americans. I know the "folk music" he must have listened to. (I too had been wand'ring early and late . . .) I have experienced the thrill of collaborating with him numerous times as we have invited each other into our respective albums. I recall our trio arrangement of "(What a) Wonderful World" with my Paul. We met at Paul's apartment (of course). It was '77. Two extraordinary artists were giving me the gifts of their vocals and guitar parts for my album *Watermark*. I must have done something right. What is memorable today is the ease and efficiency with which we three found our harmonies. There was a mutual musical sensibility and a serious mutual respect.

James is so fine. His exactitude with the Note is simple impeccable musicianship. Call it his refinement or the civility of intelligent life. Hear the innate dignity of James's tribute song to Martin Luther King Jr. ("Shed a Little Light"). Some people have a hard time with the self-consciousness of perfectionism. But I think *perfect* is the best review.

I hope he reads this little tribute of mine and recognizes what a great personal value his existence is to one of his colleagues. And I hope he breaks into another grin from ear to ear as he feels "that's why I'm here."

With James Taylor, 1997

April 17, 1990. *Sports Illustrated* covers my walk. Tom Dunkel, the writer. Nebraska.

I think of Dunkel thinking: What is Garfunkel thinking as he walks this part? Okay I think of Breughel, the painter, the elder, the sixteenth century. And Pico della Mirandola.

*

NEW YORK CITY. PLAZA HOTEL.

> Sanford Greenberg came to my fiftieth
>   birthday.
> He helped the hostess plan the ball.

He made all the people he spoke to feel his
    light.

He spoke to the group about David and
    Jonathan, honored his blindness and
riffed on the Godfather, told all the people
    How powerfully Arthur did right.

I, in back, abuzz, aloof, was enchanted,
    hand in pocket, leaning against the
doorjamb. I heard myself praised for not
    discarding loyalties and moving on.
I took the compliment.

I let him call me angel singer
    and felt myself connected to the race;
I kiss you for all the years of supporting me
    In truth, I bask in the embrace.

*

It wasn't Monet, it was France;
It's not what we say but the dance we're in—
Therein lies the mysterious glue
    and the printed page I paint for you.

*

MAY 14, 1998. NOW I BEGIN TO WALK ACROSS
EUROPE, IRELAND TO ISTANBUL.

It's the not exactly knowing of the way—
   the map thrown away,
     no thruway near—
that makes the setting sun the guide
   and makes the setting come alive.

               *

Out of the airport, over the Shannon divide,
I started to walk across Europe with only a
       prayer—
Hold me and keep me down to the Dardanelles;
   Into that other air—carry me there.

County Clare, fair weather in the dells
A lover's excursion, a lyrical Limerick song—
A merry man sang in the very middle of May
   In Arthur's Quay, inviting me along.

Here I belong to the road, and I rode my
       way
Through golden hills, green orchards rolling
     down;
Ireland in upland atmosphere.
      And so I came to Tipperary town.

       After the rule of survival must be
       People's passionate need to feel free.

Now let the Walker fall into a clockwork
   groove.

Fifty-three paces a minute shall be my gait.
Every two minutes, a tenth of a mile
I set this date: Nineteen hundred and
    ninety-eight.

Let the millennium wait, and let Clonmel by
Lead me beside the waters of Suir (SURE) so
    clear.
SHEHECHEYANU, bless me, O Lord, bless my feet
Thanks for sustaining my life and for bringing
    me here.

Ever so near to Ulysses in my conceit
He left Turkey after the Trojan fight
Against his tide my fantasies secretly yearn—
So I return to Byzantium tonight.

        We all know destination's call;
        How you make your way is all.

Identify your pleasure in the land—
Notice the knoll, see tincture of pink in the
    tree;
Queen Anne's lace is in your face to smell
Tell of BOREEN beauty bountifully.

Partake of the verb "to be," for all is well
Even the I.R.A. can go visit their moms.
What Guinness stirs in the breast of every
    dragoon
Breath itself returns in full bloom and becalms.

Lay down your arms, the harbor calls you
soon.
Drop your shoulder blades. What's in a name?
What's Celtic, what's Gaelic? All garlic in
Irish stew—
O Land of Yeats and Joyce and of poverty's
shame

It's emigration's broke your heart
And tore your families apart.

With Jack Nicholson and Warren Beatty, c. 1976

VII

I'm on a tear with my newborn son.
Kim is a kite.
I have climbed the string from earth to her.
And now we fly together.

Margaret Ashley helps us.
She rocks our boy in the rocker that Laurie
    designed.
Faith like a feather supports my love and I.
Clouds of good fortune, some stacked and
    heaped with silver-shaded caves, go by.
Aloft in love in a lucky breeze.

*

Although we have a baby, I haven't changed.
I still am in your power.
My brilliant lights would still go out
    if you would turn away.
    A leaden heart would follow me about
    and everything I say or sing
    would be a flightless thing.

I still desire you.
Please be kind to the victim of your charms.

I still need to see you
    turn to appleblossom in my arms.

Let our cup run over.
It wasn't for only the sunny days
    that I promised my love to you,
        but till time and tides are through,
    my love.
I haven't changed. My love is true.

*

I have sung for creatures all my life.
It started with humans in fifty-one.
People heard the bird in my throat and
    I was so happy to make the sound.
Word of mouth was meager, but I
    heard the gift and I went with it.
Married in the synagogue to echo and
    the minor key, I sang ancient melodies
        in the Main Street temple in Queens.

Many years later I sang for cows.
As I walked the country, there they were
On a hill
Looking at me.
So I sang to them
And they gathered round.
I give them the old vibrato.
The sound is sincere and the love of
    connection is deep.

I belt out a beautiful "Ol' Man River."
Many eyes widen.
One creature's cryin'
I AM "feared o' dyin'."

*

My life is a brimming lake,
   a lake that runneth over;
      What break in the rim?
This is the day when flow was set in motion.
Around what hill did contentment spill?

THE '90S WERE ABOUT RAISING A SON AND TOURING
THE WORLD WITH A FOUR-MAN BAND. THE TWO
CAME TOGETHER, IN '97, WITH THE RELEASING OF

Kim, Art, and Arthur Junior, 7 minutes old, 1990

TWO ALBUMS: MY NINTH SOLO, *ACROSS AMERICA—THE CONCERT AT ELLIS ISLAND*, AND THE SONY WONDER ALBUM, *SONGS FROM A PARENT TO A CHILD*, MY TENTH.

> *My darling son, I want you to know Music, Melody, a thing called a Song, and this thrill that I get in my throat—Singing. Your Daddy's work is making things—with all the beauty and care I have. I surprise myself when I make these things. I see who I am in the shape I make. It's a silver Disc and I made it for you. Know me, my son. Love life through its gifts.*
> *—Daddy*

*

FEBRUARY 14, 1997. TO KIM,

Because I count your love divine,
   my heart is yours and yours mine.
And since yours is the sweetest heart,
   I call you sweetheart—
      I am your counterpart—
         and you're my valentine.

*

WALES

Why not play with words again
What else is there to do?

Lean on winter's western wind
And let it pull me through.

Wales across the southern shore
Pembroke to Pendine
To Laugharne and to Dylan's inspired pen
I'll write another nine.

Here in the mercy of his means am I,
A pebble in the religious stream,
A tribute in the deep heart's core,
My peripatetic dream.

O Earth—you are too wonder-filled
I walk the way that God has willed.

East to England, hills unfold,
Behind me, the Irish Sea;
Off to my right, beyond Cornwall and Devon
Brittany, Normandy parallel me.

What's in a field? What is Wales?
Indian takeout? The Carpenter's Arms?
Undulation uncontrolled,
The house-high hay of her farms.

Under Cymru's* leaden skies
I forge my chain of days—

*

* Pronounced "Cumry."

ENGLAND TO FRANCE

Flying is breathing. I stand on the deck in the back of the ferry from Poole to Cherbourg. The noon sun shines on our departure. Hungry gulls again. They waft between wing beats. The glide is my model, my Plato's Ideal. Descending notes sung in a sigh.

*

Kathryn IS the month of May,
All the days belong to her;
Baby's breath becomes her hair
And everywhere the lilacs stir.

Mother's Day commemorates,
But all the dates proclaim her worth:
Renaissance of Earth named with
The Twenty-fifth—her very birth!

All the swollen, sap-sweet smell
Of hill and dell are pale and dim
Beside her fragrant exhale . . .
Spring's her trail. May IS Kim.

PARC MONCEAU, PARIS
APRIL 30, 1997

*

I BOUGHT A PIN AT TIFFANY AND GAVE IT TO KIM
AT CHRISTMAS.

Aloft in space amid fire and ice,
     on a ball in orbit with a clockwise spin,
In the land of the loon and of succulent rice
     is the city known as St. Paul's twin.

There beside Excelsior
     my lover sits amongst her kin:
While under the family Christmas tree
     my love resides within a pin.

*

That sunny crimson, those lips, her tousled hair,
the attitude. I'm a sucker when the sun shines
out. . . . No amethyst could tempt her secret soul
forsworn to love . . . worthy of Aquitaine and
rainy days that she could tell of . . .
     I took her dancing to the Sweethearts' Ball
on Friday night. I looked her over: the cut of
her dress, the way she teased her hair—she was
beautiful.
     And so we danced to unchained melody . . .
just for the thrill of holding her on the floor. (I
sang for you when I let them pull me onstage.)
We were all the rage in our own reviews that
night—lost in limelight . . . luminous . . . divine.
The moon was bright, you were mine, that sunny
Valentine.

*

FRANCE. FIFTH LEG OF EUROWALK

These are the fields I've driven across so many
times before. The nineteenth of August. The
northern view. Miraculous sun. Finally alone, I
write to you: Love rules my life.

A thousand feet above the English Channel
coast—Cherbourg. Host to the haunting memory
of indigo and dusty rose and times I rode on
the Continent . . . burning autumn leaves in late
September . . . aroma in a biker's wind. Then late
for school, I would tear myself from France.

And now I reenter the spell—on foot, hushedly,
and with reverence for the trance: Stendhal,
Balzac, Debussy, and Ravel, Voltaire, Molière,
Robespierre and Racine, Rodin, Renoir, Proust
and Monet, Camille Corot and the road ahead
D87, a two-lane blacktop south and east to
Byzantium.

To be with Jean Rhys in Paris, or to drink
with Joyce when he came through that town.
To tour with Montaigne and Bridget Bardot,
Le Corbusier's Ronchamp, Azay-le-Rideau. O I
could tell of days of intoxication with France: an
orchard in Aurillac, curve of the river Yonne, the
grass we danced on at Rambouillet behind the
king's château . . . "Here, There and Everywhere"
had just been released . . . I sang at the old
Olympia before they tore it down. I rode in the

rain on a bike by the Porte de Clignancourt. We
sang at night on the Boulevard St. Michel and at
a racetrack where Degas painted and a hundred
thousand French came for each of two nights. I
know antique simplicity in the Ardèche mountains,
peace in the Midi, brandy and moonlight at Les
Deux Alpes skiing with *les étudiants* . . . we
sang on the boardwalk with Kathy in Nice under
the stars in '65 and used the francs we made
to eat. The Frenchman I most got to know was
Rousseau—I see him as an orphan boy in the high
Savoy.

I have seen my own life pass in France since
'62 in old Cambray my own Swann's Way, blasé to
the Norman land today I muse: How like Odette
was Laurie Bird—naughty and gorgeous.

*

My wife and I and our eight-year-old attended a
Buddhist meeting with our guards up, down, and
in-between. He was rebellious, she was courageous,
and I was wondering what it would mean.

The Junior Pioneers met in Room 306. The
group leader offered the image of leaves that fall
but return; our son begged to differ—what's gone
is gone—but I was a skeptic in my turn.

Then I had to leave (to record in Orlando)
while the group went to garden in Union
Square: I called from the airport to hear him
triumphant—he had planted fourteen tulips there!

Kathryn and Arthur Jr.

*

From February 1989 to January 1999 I read 312 books. These 26 books stand out:

Theodore Dreiser, *An American Tragedy* (1925)
Sylvia Plath, *The Bell Jar* (1963)
Thomas Mann, *The Magic Mountain* (1927)
Rachel Carson, *Silent Spring* (1962)
Marcus Aurelius, *Meditations* (AD 177)
H. G. Wells, *A Short History of the World* (1922)

Swami Prabhavananda, *The Sermon on the Mount According to Vedanta* (1963)

Hermann Hesse, *Demian* (1919)

Stanley Coren, *The Left-Hander Syndrome* (1992)

The Random House Dictionary of the English Language (1966)

Franz Kafka, *The Trial* (1920)

Daniel Defoe, *A Journal of the Plague Year* (1724)

Jean Rhys, *After Leaving Mr. Mackenzie* (1931)

Henry Kissinger, *Diplomacy* (1994)

Robert D. Kaplan, *Balkan Ghosts* (1993)

Gustave Flaubert, *Flaubert in Egypt* (1850)

Charles and Mary Lamb, *Tales from Shakespeare* (1807)

Keith B. Richburg, *Out of America* (1997)

Patrick Süskind, *Perfume* (1986)

Ralph Ellison, *Invisible Man* (1952)

Jimmy Webb, *Tunesmith* (1998)

Fyodor Dostoevsky, *The Devils* (1871)

Émile Zola, *Germinal* (1885)

Peter Gay, *The Enlightenment: The Science of Freedom* (1969)

John Updike, *Rabbit, Run* (1960)

Nathaniel Hawthorne, *The House of the Seven Gables* (1851)

*

I HAVE PSORIASIS. PERIODICALLY I GO TO THE MAYO CLINIC AND LIVE IN PAJAMAS.

I'm back in the school for skin,
     In for another three weeks;
Tar all over my body,
     The patient heals, the writer seeks.

Are we like leaves that come and go?
My boy calls our home CAMP CHIPPERCOW
     and his family, CHIPPERCATTLE

Rochester, Minnesota,
     Serioustown, USA.
Worried wives in elevators,
     hooked-up husbands in the hall.

And I'm just here with psoriasis,
     luckiest of all.

A tide-me-over, help for hangin' on
Silently, the Stalker in the streets
     pronounces judgments through
          the town on the frightened
               population that it meets
                    . . . ye shall mend,
                         but you

                              *

I sit
and I look
at the picture I took
of our beautiful son . . .

In the immensity—
is us,
the two of us,
onlookers
of what we are
and what we have created

In awe together,
my love and I
step back from the picture
at Christmastime, 1994.

What other wonders
might we humbly
shepherd
ashore?

*

Then, in 1996, my wife was diagnosed with breast cancer. For the second time, life stopped.

VIII

To Sanford, dearer than dear.

   I am your long-lost love, your grandmother,
your Yiddish-kite, the light in the old green
house, the soul of your early days. I am the *tallis*
you wear since then. You can be the rabbi, Moses
Haddas. Dear God, let me be the cantor in prayer
again.

*

No, you can't blame the elm disease on us as
   such
—it's Dutch. But the ravage hasn't reached
this original hippie sixty miles west of the
   Mississippi.
Here under the magnificent spread of a
   hundred-foot vase,
I am thinking of the fork in the trunk, an
   early divorce.
Trunks packed like trees, they grew divergent,
poised between the reach of the leaves for
   open air
and the pull of the partner*—a perpetual "V,"

* THIS IS PAUL SIMON

a devoted duality, balm of balance, rapturous
    realm,

a remaining American Elm.

*

To my Kathryn

The beauty of a tree is its integrity.
Like humanfolk, it's whole when it's in balance.

Anchored underground, the roots are daily
        drinking
    where nectar of the earth is sunk.
Up above, avenues of branches are dancing in
        the air—
    not anywhere but massed in equal weight
    around a center pole, the trunk.

There in the distance, a spreading oak is on
        display for me.
I see it two-dimensionally—
    a plane of woods on a stick, a counterpoise.
And I delight to see, among my joys,
    how the rotating plane holds the picture as
        I draw near.
    The picture of an Eastern Dancer—
    a hundred arms in balance on her toe—
    my bodhisattva!

But now I lie with my lover beneath a maple
        tree.

She and I look up to see a six-foot hole in the
     trunk—
   a gash filled in with tarry pitch some years
     ago.

We recognize, we three, the flaws of
     vulnerability—
   fault lines of experience.

The maple carries our eye above the wound
     to the sky.
   (What does it matter that weather harms?)
Before it, spreads the perfect canopy of
     green.
Branches dancing in the brilliant balanced
     scene—
   integrity intact.
The tree has absorbed its history. Leaves shine.

Its wholeness, our epiphany, my love's and
     mine.
Sisters in arms, we lie before the bodhisattva's
     perfect ninety-nine!

*

Christmas 1997. In this holy time of year, I bow
before you, Kathryn dear, transcendent o'er your
trial of fear. For unto few the task is given—like
the Ascension's risen Christ—to know the Valley
and pay the price, to pass through the Shadow
and be born twice!

*

TO SANFORD

To slip from the shore and swim in the
  widening stream
   of our history once more starlit in the
   mystery
of the mutual love we store against the
   night—

*

It's the end of the day, the evening is near, the
first of December, the end of the year. It's
the end of the decade, an era of mystery; even
the twentieth century's history. A new thousand
years starts in thirty-one days, and I can feel
ten thousand years ago—vertigo—accessible today.
But my love for Arthur Junior (expressed here in
rhyme) goes way beyond this span of time.

*

More than your teammates, it's who guards you
that carries the bond. Who was appointed or self-
appointed to watch your every move.

*

I GRIPPED THE PIANO AS I SANG ONSTAGE. IT WAS
A ROCKY TRIP FROM THE SOUTHERN TIP OF CHILE

ACROSS THE DRAKE PASSAGE TO THE ANTARCTIC
PENINSULA ON THE *OCEAN EXPLORER*. IT WAS THE
LAST WEEK OF DECEMBER 1999. THE GARFUNKELS
WERE LITTLE EARTH ANGELS AS WE WALKED AMONG
THE PENGUINS AT THE CLOSE OF THE MILLENNIUM.

*

MAY 2001. WALKING THROUGH NORMANDY TO
PARIS.

My son is here to remind me of my
   original nature. Singing is the same.
Being fine, holding to goodness
   so much as to be divinely touched,
adored at the door where we came in.

Four-thirty at Chavenay, I resume my way,
   my seventh stay on the road to the east.
I walk for simplicity, to empty out,
   to come about with my sails,
to reflect, as a boy, the original joy of spring.

Moral tone, moral fiber, word of honor,
   pitch ring true.

Here I walk. Free. In authenticity. Alive
   to the ages of man,
to the moon on the tide, the original spin—
   France's rolling waves of what has been. . . .
I will go back to junior high, to innocence,
   to see my son come in.

*

Like fingerprints that are unique, no two
faces on earth are the same. But you? Surely
I've seen a few of you before, six at least this
year. Uncanny doubles surround me. Familiar
physiognomy.

*

Like a knight, an itinerant warrior, I will lay me
down sometimes on a massage table. Out come the
words aromatherapy bodywork drink more water
and one hundred twenty-five dollars please. I let
them have me and go to pleasure, to relaxation,
and it feels so good.

Last Sunday in Asheville, a hippie masseuse
came to my hotel room before the show to do me.
I never see hippies around anymore, but there
was the incense, the talent, the attitude. There,
the language: "When Jerry died" means Deadhead,
and her mantra was "It's all good."

"It's all good . . . It's all good . . . Is it all
good?" I knew what she meant—spine and idealism
thrive on a push. (Have I given my heart, my hips
to a slightly older wiser Jenna Bush?) It's turn-
of-the-century transcendence for her; a tentative
stance of dependence for me.

But is it all love when push comes to shove?

Now she packs up while I must get on to

the sound check. "If you would, could you
please?" . . . Suddenly she's lost her car keys.
(I'd rather feel late than loss if I could.) In
silence, she burns. I turn to wood (is it *all*
good?), to stone, the adjective, Appalachian,
alone at the end of spring, to full-grown
antipathy, moral tone turned mush—a slightly
older colder Mr. Bush.

*

IN SEPTEMBER 2001, AMERICA IS HIT. THE WORLD
TRADE CENTER'S TWIN TOWERS FALL. WE ARE
SHOCKED BY OUR VIOLABILITY. NATIONALISM BE
DAMNED AND ALL THOUGHTS ABOUT IT. MY LOVE
FOR AMERICA IS REAL.

Perhaps if I steal from Thomas Wolfe
    and give him his proper due—
not the "man in full" but the "homeward
        angel"
    —he might reappear for you.

Then see him up there where the Rockies
rise, his legs dangling over the ledge above
Denver, eight thousand feet in the air.
Before him, the plains, behind, the Pacific,
stars coming out on a summer's night, and
everywhere the twilight falls on America.

To the right is Amarillo, beyond it the
Astros at play, over my shoulder, Seattle,
over the other beyond the Great Canyon,
gas fumes and fast food mix with the smell
of L.A. Hear the blues parade across the
stage. Up from New Orleans into Chicago,
see all the clusters of light beyond. Follow
the fashion of rock 'n' roll—St. Louie to
Cleveland to Philly to bond the nation's soul
with music in its cars.

And in our hearts love of the physical
entity. America. Identity in doubt. We can't
go home again, so we're runaway vagabonds,
lost in twilight, wondering what we're about.

—9/11/2001

*

SOON AFTER, I CO-WROTE "PERFECT MOMENT"
FOR MY 11TH SOLO ALBUM, *EVERYTHING WAITS TO
BE NOTICED.*

When Simon and Garfunkel received the
Grammy Lifetime Achievement Award (2002),
this was my speech to industry colleagues:

"I am enormously proud of our body of work,
Paul's and mine. My whole life has been deeply
enriched by the musical gifts of this neighbor

of mine from Kew Gardens Hills I never would
have had this career if Paul Simon wasn't such
a magnificent rhythm guitar player. His grooves
underlie all our music. Think of 'Mrs. Robinson,'
of 'Scarborough Fair'—it was always Paul on
acoustic guitar. Then think of 'Bridge Over
Troubled Water'—yes I am proud of my vocal
performance, but the song is Paul's. Is there
any writer in our time with such beauty and
poignancy of heart and mind? I doubt that
anyone has received gifts to rival the songs he
put through my singing voice.

"I miss that earlier, sweeter America—it was
almost a lifetime ago when you imagined us
today, lost in our overcoats, sharing a park
bench quietly . . . and now we share in this
Lifetime Achievement Award for work we fussed
over endlessly in the recording studio. To me it
comes down to this: one and one can coexist, or
add up to two, or in our case, they can affect
each other like electric energy, resulting in this
Grammy honor tonight. In the words of Nat King
Cole—sort of the door I came in on—Love is the
thing!"

*

Now the moment I awaited has arrived: I leave
my Paris hotel to go southeast across Europe. If
it's one part east for each one part south—then
I go to Lausanne; if it's three parts east to two

parts south—Lucerne; I choose two parts east to three parts south—Lyon.

*

Dear Jack,

   You are the last great intellectual—lover of ideas. You crave connection but like Moby Dick in a shallow pond, you withdraw to the sea. I, your friend (without harpoon) see your winking eye on the long cruise. I have tracked you for half our lives—from frolic through fashion to father. Like Gleason, you are the Great One, a truly fine Artist.

*

Enough of the virtual world—
   I walk for tangibility, to see
the newest green and the space between.
I know the life of a town is in the
   interpersonal dramas of its people,
and that all I see is the set.
But at Combs-la-Ville,
   forty kilometers south-southeast of Paris,
I have passed through all the furniture.
Now an arcade of actual trees,
   a hundred tall sycamores,
makes a canopy for the groom in love.

   and I delight to sense them
sense each other, almost touching,
   leaving room above.

With Mort Lewis, our manager, c. 1983

*

My son is my conscience. Mired in business,
shredded in rage, lost in a sea of inane
flattery. . . . He makes me be a better man.

*

A town is temptation. I shall not stop.
I'll follow the crops in the field across
   France,
entranced by the shape of the land.
I go with the sweeping broad line
of the landscape, a man enhanced,
increased, south and east.

The zephyr, the zebra, the zodiac and I
glide on the two-lane blacktop.
Two twenty-two in the afternoon,
April seven, two thousand two,
Montereau centre ahead.

Forty-five miles below Paris.
Call the prince's carriage, my feet,
elite among all modes of transport.
DO NOT STREAM THE EARTH. LIFE IS NOT
A SCAN. Dwell on the dell and
the worth of man as best you can.

Let the shoulders give up.
Let the floor of the belly fall down.
Breathe in and out three steps apiece,
then four, then five and up to twelve.
Do one hundred steps (or fifty paces)
a minute till the end of facts:
to transcend—relax.

And behold: the beautiful confluence
of the Yonne and the Seine.
(He travels farthest who knowest not where
    or when.)

                    *

The sky is like mercury.
The heavens mercurial.
The earth is bathed in mercurochrome
    and mercy is the cure.

I walk alone in Burgundian wonder:
    to Byzantium still, with the world
        so insecure?

*

    When books were new in Gutenberg time
up the river Rhine in Mainz, in a printer's
shop on the press it read, "Let the Word
go forth; a new consensus is born." Then
they spread it around the Continent from
Germany to Paris, from Venice to Lyon—
serving Italy and Spain for the reading-
prone—it was in Lyon where you caught
the early train to Cicero, St. Augustine,
and all that praise of God that's in between
the page and man, if you were a book fan.

    Maybe it's like recorded sound a hundred
years from the start—Gutenberg is Edison,
and I am a man of middle age in 1552. The
Renaissance is in decline but these old eyes of
mine have seen my own devotions of the heart,
like an early master, play a part in the history
of the art.

    Now the printer comes to town,
unknown. Typeset faces trademark serifs
characters *italic* and apprentice to no man.
O Sacré Coeur, as it were, O *Font* of every
blessing plead my lower case above: though

I am prone to wander and to leave the God
I love, say that I walked to Lyon in January
just for the thrill, at the groin of Europe, if
you will.

                                        *

*To bathe in the fountain you must take off
your clothes.*

Stage Life, so much less than it seems to be.
Spoken for and available, vulnerable to cant,
raked amid rivers of instrument cables,
even the floor is aslant.

We're caterers, the band and I,
we serve courses from "El Condor" to Marvin
     Gaye,
the soundmen, the haulers, each in our way
pray for moments of truth.

We set up the lighting truss, go through the
     sound check,
look for the ensemble to fuse. Listening is
     everything.
Give it all up to the Gods and then get out
     of town . . .
But first stick around a while after the show:

They're loading the speakers into the truck,
     miles to go

. . . I turn to the faces I sing for—I hear it,
   in the deep
heart's core, there at the stage door. I see it,
   their glittering eyes are gay!
Fountain spray.
Each in her way went awandering while we
   played.
I personally prayed to the "verb" all night,
to the re'verb, the echo, the wetness of sound.

I know my call. It's all around me as I sign my
   name.
I feel the heart jump—all eyes dewy,
within a band of fans, I stand in makeup,
naked at the pump.

IX

I am Arthur, what is art? What's an Artie at my age? Show business as real life? If I'm to be a Garfunkel, isn't God a joker? Kim is Kathryn. Kathryn is Kim. The only truth I know is her. Her health is stable now, thank God.

I've done a thousand concerts with my four-piece band. I learned to perform without Paul. Concert halls, casinos, with orchestras, inside and outside America. My mother's gone, James is twelve. My brother Jules is soon to die. the friendly fellow who picks up our pizza is now in the Oval Office.

And suddenly Simon & Garfunkel fall back in step together again. Nobody needed the money. But once you hold a rehearsal, you drift back into that magical, effortless blend. Where does it come from? From seeing things alike in junior high. From laughing at Nichols and May.

*

Come and watch over us,
May we yet be blessed

Forgive ourselves
And lay it all to rest.

*

Camogli, east of Genoa, along the coast beyond
Sori. Election Day six days away—the mystery of
how we allowed George Bush. And as he reigned
it was Hitler explained. We should've known that
self-righteousness only inflamed. "God on our
side" rocks the world. Dylan knew and we used
to know, forty years ago. Am I still on my way
to Istanbul? Aren't all bets off with Bush?

The sea paces. Death is waiting, shimmering

*

From sushi to sashimi,
    from a walk to a jog,
France becomes a trainer's ramp.
Summer cannot wane or age
    the walker's bead on a new stage.

The heart moves in from the left.
The Pitted Kettle begins to make
    a sound surrounding us,
        resounding to the Evermore,
        another thaw—
I am in awe.
I forgive.

*

10 REASONS WHY I AM IN AWE OF MY WIFE:

1) She has the silhouette of a nubile Egyptian princess.
2) Three billionaires are loyal to her.
3) She never cooks a bad meal.
4) When she tires of seeing Provence on the back of a motorcycle, she falls asleep forward (clicking helmets), not back.
5) She tells the mayor of NYC to have a heart about taxi drivers' wages, and she uses a one-minute photo op with the president at the White House to ask George about his global bearings.
6) She possesses a considerable range of great kisses.
7) She can emit a living object out of her body which is twelve times larger than the aperture of emission. (In man's terms: like passing a gerbil through the penile canal.)
8) She has transcended money, and uses it only for classes and clothes (jewelry, real estate gaining).
9) Her beauty as a mother, pure gold to me, puts the Virgin Mary into the silver.
10) She's a kickass actress, and she loves me.

*

WE SHOWCASED THE EVERLY BROTHERS, PLAYING
ARENAS IN THE USA AND IN EUROPE. WE CLOSED THE
TOUR WITH A FREE SHOW IN ROME—600,000 FANS IN
THE FAMOUS STREETS. SUMMER OF 2004.

une vie quotidienne de chansons

Now that it's over and nine hundred twenty-
two songs have been done before six hundred

Chamonix, France, 1988

eighty-eight thousand fans to show we can do
it—*all the world's a stage, a play we intuit*—I
tender my love to the Lord Almighty for letting
the notes, divinely spun, come alive each night
preponderate, allowing me to be the conduit.

*

What is a day? What's the point of it all?
We never chose our nose or the names we
      wear.
Set adrift by the gift of life, it's a pall to
      bear.

How shall I fill the morning, the night?
Spending time in rhyme or in grateful prayer?
Is it a fall through air or a sacred rite?

What if there's great regret at the end?
Does He intend to move us toward Aware?
Does it behoove us to blend the sight,
   the flight and the plight in each day's
     share of delight?

*

It might have rained last night. The day is
fiercely beautiful. Radiant sun falls on interfolding
hills climbing to the spine of Tuscany, La Lima to
Pistoia and to Brunelleschi's dome, home to art
majors like me, a walker in the dells (here, church

bells), faint Etruscan images only Carrara marble
tells in gorgeous morning air. Two eyes over
Italy, ridge in the Mediterranean floor. Before me,
shells on the Adriatic shore, then down to the
Dardanelles.

*

BEAU DANIEL GARFUNKEL, OUR SECOND SON, WAS
BORN TODAY, OCTOBER 5, 2005. THEN BROUGHT TO
THE HOTEL BEL-AIR.

Enter the second son.
Into the Land of a Thousand Gardeners.
Into the open wind and the mortal wound.

Simon and Garfunkel at the Roman Colosseum onstage, screen 2004

*

My notion of the place that awaits us beyond the world is like my memory of a certain synagogue on a hill—vague. It was down our block, into the reeds, around the lake, where you climbed a hill to a shimmering temple, alabaster sky, June in the afternoon. The light, the lectern, the emerald shade . . . my brother Jules runs on ahead.

*

. . . remorse, regret, shame, and wasted time . . .

*

AT THE START OF THE 21ST CENTURY, THE WHOLE WORLD AND ITS COLLECTIVE CONSCIOUSNESS HAD MOVED TO FEAR—IF YOU ARE UNSURE OF IT, FEAR IT. IF YOU SEE SOMEONE SINGING WITH AN IPOD IN THE AIRPORT, IS IT YELLOW ALERT? ONCE AMERICA NEEDED AN ACT OF PROVOCATION TO INVADE ANOTHER COUNTRY, NOW ONLY SUSPICION AND PARANOIA ARE REQUIRED. ALL THE FORA OF REASON AND CARE, ALL EFFORT TO UNDERSTAND DIFFERENCES AMONG NATIONS, AND THEIR SHADES OF GRAY, SEEM TO HAVE BEEN SWEPT ASIDE BY THE SECOND BUSH ADMINISTRATION. SIMPLISTICALLY, SHOCKINGLY, IT ALL BECAME A WAR OF OIL AND RELIGION (MUHAMMAD VS. MCDONALD'S) AND IT DROPPED CIVILIZATION BACK FIVE HUNDRED YEARS. "IF YOU FEAR IT, ATTACK IT."

Jacques Barzun or anyone
who talks to me like him
    wins my sympathy in this decadent age.

What has "learn to earn" meant
but a fight against civilized discernment?

Is it that "time thins out things"?
Does the quality of life lessen
    with human increase?

If it all dilutes through the centuries,
    then from Rembrandt's soulful portrayals
        to Chartres Cathedral
            to Aquinas
                to Greek ARETÉ
                    people have seen their better day.

*

My poetry bits are organs. What is the least
connective tissue that sets them in a body?

*

From February 1999 to January 2006 I read 179
books. These 26 books stand out:

Russell Banks, *Cloudsplitter* (1998)
Philip Roth, *American Pastoral* (1997)
Jacob Riis, *How the Other Half Lives* (1890)

A. J. P. Taylor, *The Struggle for Mastery in Europe, 1848–1918* (1954)

Alfred Lansing, *Endurance: Shackleton's Incredible Voyage* (1959)

Jacques Barzun, *From Dawn to Decadence* (2000)

Jakob Walter, *The Diary of a Napoleonic Foot Soldier* (1850)

Adolf Hitler, *Mein Kampf* (1926)

Artie Shaw, *The Trouble with Cinderella* (1952)

Paramahansa Yogananda, *Autobiography of a Yogi* (1946)

Elizabeth Gaskell, *Wives and Daughters* (1866)

Upton Sinclair, *The Jungle* (1905)

Jean Rhys, *Sleep It Off Lady* (1976)

Harold Nicolson, *Good Behavior* (1955)

Lucien Febvre and Hanri-Jean Martin, *The Coming of the Book* (1958)

Charles Bukowski, *Post Office* (1971)

Majid Tehranian and Daisaku Ikeda, *Global Civilization: A Buddhist-Islamic Dialogue* (2003)

Robert Caro, *The Years of Lyndon Johnson: Master of the Senate* (2002)

Aesop, *The Complete Fables* (c. 550 BC)

Groucho Marx, *Love, Groucho* (1992)

Bob Dylan, *Chronicles*, Vol. 1 (2004)

Laurens van der Post, *A Story Like the Wind* (1972)

Laurence Bergreen, *As Thousands Cheer: The Life of Irving Berlin* (1990)

Anthony Trollope, *The Way We Live Now* (1873)

Émile Zola, *The Debacle* (1870)
Edith Wharton, *The Age of Innocence* (1920)

*

Today I'll judge my books by their covers.
I'll watch a pot, count unhatched chicks,
I'll fix the unbroken, hold secret gods divine.

A thousand fine soldiers, resplendent in
    their jacket designs, are lined in shelves
        in my aerie—
All the noble sentiments quilled,
Cry for all the milk that's spilled,
Let the unaware buyer be sold—
If the book cover glitters, it's gold;
I'll make a Top Forty polled for pretty veneers,
    how the book appears, and how it feels
        to hold and be held the whole night
            through . . .
Today I'll do exactly what you're not
    supposed to do.

*

Take the word "PRECIOUS"—
it loses its value as we marginalize "SWEET."

We push away poignancy. Nothing's profound.
And "PRETTY" things, like furry slippers,
are for the effete.

Take opals in a brimming cup—
what would you say if you saw some
now that "AWESOME"'s used up?
Is there wholeness still in "WHOLESOME"
or did it go *McCall's?* IS there anything left
at all that calls to God?

Here's a letter from Precious Knudsen.
I haven't met her but she interviewed here
for a nanny position about a week ago.
Slowly I open the envelope.

—I heard from the agency that you do
not think I am the right fit . . .

O Precious Knudsen, what's in a name?
If life had no language, would it be the
    same?

*

We played a small park band shell in Leipzig
the sixth of July. I opened with "Homeward
Bound" and went through fifteen tunes. The
rain had stopped, the roof leak ceased. After
"Bridge Over Troubled Water," my son came out
for "Cecilia." He greeted the audience in German,
introduced himself in German, he thanked them
for waiting in the rain. He hoped they would
enjoy "Mr. Blue" as much as he did. He wore his
daddy's black-and-white Elvis shirt. He looked to

At the U.S. Open tennis tournament, September 8, 2002

be one very attractive pop star. James Arthur was a hit.

After the show we were leaving with the driver. There were fans at the gate. We stopped to greet them and sign autographs. I, in back, shared the contact—such love—with two dozen East Germans. James, in front at the window, was telling this lovely girl, smiling up at his eyes, what his email address is. She's coming to tomorrow's show in Munich! Her name is Emily. The flaming torch of rock 'n' roll is passing from father to son.

Big free show at the Roman Colosseum,
    six hundred thousand Italians,
    a year and a week ago.

I walk the Siena road today
    through middle Italy.

Little we know of the way of things,
    of the Buddha's art—
    of what will connect
    and what will remain apart.

*

IN ROME, IN THE VILLA BORGHESE, IS A MUSEUM WITH
SCULPTURES BY THE GREAT BERNINI.

   See Daphne trapped in trees. The myth has
her running from Apollo, turning into a tree
at the moment of his touch. Hence, forever
elusive. . . . But I see Arthur chasing Kathryn
trapped inside the trunk of a willow tree, her
history. At his touch, the bark falls away. The
young sculptor, Michelangelo, began one day with
a block of stone. As he found the *Pietà* within, so
I embrace the emerging Kathryn.

*

I was her love pest.
Like aphids in the garden.
Mold on her bloom.
I was fungus underneath her nail.
Crust in her eyelashes.
Trust in the atmosphere.
Dust on the pictures of places we've been.
I'm her old bed linen.
The thrust of the argument.
Honey for tea in a bear.
I'm the horn in her side
    cornucopia.
I am her underwear.
Solder and weld.
Fused in our children.
    Behold and be held.

*

Darling Kim. I AM your dream. I AM the man
you think I am. You DID divine my spirit quite
rightly when you were little. Now we mature.
Both our inner spirits are "busied over" with our
lives' events. As cataracts becloud the eye with
age, so the soul—the core of one's self—must stay
aware. The flame of one's life is 100 percent
flame for as long as it burns.

I BURN for you, baby Kim, while I live. There
is no arc, no peak then fade. I am so close to
you, you feel so attached to my heart, wherever
I go . . . darling, your nature—when you come to

me of a sudden, in the little village of Laglio, on
Lake Como, is divine. So I AM on the other end
of your powerful thoughts of me. I DO receive
your prayers through the air.

This love of ours is very beautiful to me. Time
polishes it beautifuller in spite of the admixture
of my aging crust, thickening bark of the trunk
of a tree, maturing and spreading itself with air
and forgiveness sooo beautifully. The tree of us is
getting a little big now, darling. Dancing in the
wind, it says: "I embrace

*

Paul's mother, Belle, dies. June 15, 2007. This
is the age of dying—the end of June, abundant
fecundity. Laurie Bird, Rose Garfunkel, Belle
Simon. . . . Why do they leave just then? Is it
a showdown for them—a fork in a larger road?
Keenly, with alienation, do they say to the ripest
earth: "Today, you go your way . . ."? (Or is it
just a clock run down?)

*

To Paul, from Art: We're out under the stars
now, the harbor we came from is gone from view.

*

When the biological imperative to continue the
race is achieved and the need to create is done,
birds can lose their song, color is extraneous,

and briefs become boxers. Why stick around?
Because the world needs delight to care to grow

*

To chase cachet is to unleash the cliché
and turn kitsch into so much quiche,
as when K___ casually mentioned
her friend Rajneesh—
Though the namedrop was blatant
I teased out her pretension instead
until The Bogwan was said.

THE ACTUAL PARIS SOLO SHOW
8 P.M., MARCH 21, 2007
Olympia Theatre

FIRST HALF—40 MINUTES

EL CONDOR PASA
AMERICAN TUNE
AND SO IT GOES
A HEART IN NEW YORK
CRYING IN THE RAIN
THE BOXER
SOME ENCHANTED EVENING
PERFECT MOMENT
SCARBOROUGH FAIR

SECOND HALF—50 MINUTES

MRS. ROBINSON
HOMEWARD BOUND
BRIGHT EYES
QUIET NIGHTS
ALL I KNOW
REAL EMOTIONAL GIRL
BRIDGE OVER TROUBLED WATER

CECILIA
KATHY'S SONG
THE SOUND OF SILENCE

GOODNIGHT MY LOVE
WHAT'S GOING ON

*

We have a three-foot-diameter plastic globe
    that sits on the floor of our bedroom.
The countries are colored. The ocean's aqua.
These days we keep it unlit
    for little Beau's safety's sake.

Through the east window comes the
            morning sun.
The bedroom is radiant with joy,
    the Brandenburg IV is medium-loud.
Little Beau swooshes before me, pushing the
        globe
    out the door; little feet pumping strong,
he rolls the world along the tiles to the kitchen.
    It bangs into furniture. The denting is global.
I know I should take it away.

Beau and the Globe are a two-character
            play to me.
The things they do reverberate.
See Beau imitate his family of singers
    as he puts his mouth into the opening
        in the North Pole.
His one-year-old stretch gets him up and over
    and down and in, calling his tenor note
        across the earth's interior.

Now there's a big welt across the English
            Midlands,
    a round depression at Odessa, and part of
        Poland's

chipped away. (I know I must save the
world
from Beau but my discipline is undone
by the sweet conceit.)

One night I find myself embracing my
Kathryn
and allowing myself to be embraced
by the beauty of my life today.
Our hearts swell together.
Out from our feet, little Beau rolls the globe
away.

*

My son was so handsome last night, so forthright,
so earnest, so dressed to kill—dark charcoal
lightweight suit, tie all cranberry red, golden
curls, eager to learn, beautiful complexion, 15¼
the brink of change.

MARCH 31, 2006

*

I don't write bits to my firstborn son—
words would diminish my love.
Now that HE IS, I AM
a something else again,
a captive of how much I care
and unaware of time,
heart without rhyme,
my son defies defining.

The heart is a fist,
   a muscle pumping blood,
the source of the thing I feel for him:
my son is a lover with the muscle grown,
   he IS the poem and the poet's aims—
no names describe his embrace
   as wide as the human race.

                *

To my "partner's" son,
Though the challenge, the direction is as
blinding as the sun, aim toward your father's
heart and just take one baby step toward it.
A little is a lot. Let your true inner self be
warmed. His is the heart that needs to melt.
Let cracks precede the awe-full task. Then
recede, slip back, go cloudy like the weather,
whatever. But please persist before he dies.
See him as the lonely one—a poet turning
prosaic. You are the rising sun.

                *

The bedsore doctor needed someone to brace
my brother. So I came up against his back and
rotated him on his hip, while the hideous wound
was rebandaged. There, in his bed, on my elbow, I
pushed my neck and my cheek into the back of
his shoulder. I felt I belonged there—kid brother
behind his brother's wing. I held him and kissed
his neck and behind his ear. Death was present.

The smell was in his mouth—cancer was almost
done with its work. It was unprecedented that
I would hold him, here at the end of life at last.
The wound was dressed. We returned him in place.
After a time he gave an indication. I leaned my
ear to his mouth. "Is there something you need,
Jules?" I said. "Money," he said.

X

AND THESE ARE ALSO THINGS YOU THINK ABOUT:

> The great ones are the ones who mix and
>   match,
> blending contradictions. Take Jack, for example.
> We all know his spectacular vernacular.
>
> I worked with him on camera, in a dorm
>   room,
> a bedroom, a man cave. I know the exquisite
>   artist.
> I was in the room when he went to ten on the
>   scale
> of temper, take after take after take after take.
> Amidst the interior strain of sheer brilliance,
> he joked with a grip on the scaffold above us
> —fellow workers tilting lights in an industry
>   town.
> Jack straddled these realities, and rubbed his
> loves together. In the broad dissonance,
> Atlas held it up *and* scratched an itch.
> Mix it, Jack.

*

On crooner ballooner, happily to Napoli, in pretty Italy.

*

I passed through a season of dying (please God). Climbing into Frosinone on the Rome-to-Naples road, sixty or more sycamores were silently dropping their leaves, one by one, a glide. In khaki camouflage, the wet barks witness the big brown sails come down.

I thought of my mother and sighed. I thought of my brother Jules and died a little with the trees. A shady arcade, a quiet grove of letting go. Gravely, in stride, at the end of the fall, I crushed the leaves in the nave under toe.

*

**We give one-sixth their worth to those alive;
afterward—the other five.**

*

On my iPod:

Ong So Hung, Vocal Exercises I–IV, VII * **James Taylor,** Enough to Be on Your Way * **Gaia** * Ananas * Up from Your Life * Walking My Baby Back Home * **J. J. Cale,** Crying Eyes * Magnolia

* **The Everly Brothers,** That Silver Haired
Daddy of Mine * Put My Little Shoes Away *
Rocking Alone in an Old Rocking Chair * I'm
Here to Get My Baby out of Jail * Lightning
Express * Kentucky * Oh So Many Years * **Chet
Baker,** The Thrill Is Gone * But Not for Me *
Time After Time * I Get Along Without You *
There Will Never Be Another You * Look for the
Silver Lining * I've Never Been in Love Before *
Simon and Garfunkel, Old Friends / Bookends
* **Bruce Hornsby,** Song C (Instrumental) * **Art
Garfunkel,** Someone to Watch over Me * Let's
Fall in Love * You Stepped out of a Dream *
It Could Happen to You * What'll I Do * **J. J.
Cale,** Call Me the Breeze * Nowhere to Run *
The Everly Brothers, Devoted to You * Take
a Message to Mary * Let It Be Me * I Wonder
If I Care as Much * **J. J. Cale,** Crazy Mama *
Maurice Ravel, Ma Mère l'Oye Part 1 * Ma Mère
l'Oye Part 2 * Ma Mère l'Oye Part 5 * **Paul
Desmond,** Old Friends * **The Swingle Singers,**
J. S. Bach, Fugue in D Major * J. S. Bach,
Chorale in E♭ Major * J. S. Bach, Fugue #2 in
D Major * J. S. Bach, Brandenberg Concerto V,
3 * **Maurice Ravel,** *Daphnis et Chloé*, Suite
No. 2 * **Enrico Caruso,** *The Pearl Fishers* * **Nick
Holmes,** The Promise * **J. S. Bach,** Et in terra
pax * **Leon Russell,** Love's Supposed to Be That
Way * **Kenny Rankin,** Blackbird * **Lenny Bruce,**
Frank Dell * **Igor Stravinsky,** Shrovetide Fair *
James Taylor, You Can Close Your Eyes * **J. S.
Bach,** *Christmas Oratorio* duet * **Frank Sinatra,**

The House I Live In * Dylan Thomas, Fern Hill * W. B. Yeats, Blessed by Everything * Billie Holiday, Don't Explain * The Everly Brothers, So Sad * Robert Frost, Birches * W. B. Yeats, The Wild Swans at Coole * James Taylor, Another Grey Morning * Michael McDonald, Real Love * James Taylor, I've Been Wonderin' * Singers Unlimited, Have Yourself a Merry Little Christmas * Steve Reich, *Music for 18 Musicians* * James Taylor, Lookin' for Love on Broadway * W. B. Yates, Innisfree * Bill Evans, This Will Take Work * Player, Baby Come Back * Kool and the Gang, Cherish * Stephen Bishop, City Girl * Michael McDonald, I Can Let Go Now * Maia Sharp, Long Way Home * James Joyce, *Portrait of the Artist as a Young Man* * Ruth Draper, The Italian Lesson * Joni Mitchell, Wish I Had a River * Fleetwood Mac, Rhiannon * J. S. Bach, B minor Mass * James Taylor, Never Die Young * Jimmy Webb, Come Thou Fount * Paul Brady, Steal Your Heart * Jimmy Webb, Inneskillen * Paul Brady, Oh the Beauty * Let It Happen * Jimmy Webb, A Baptist Hymn * Skywriter * Stephen Bishop, That's When She Cries * Maurice Ravel, Concerto in G * Ralph Vaughan Williams, *Five Variants of Dives and Lazarus* * Claude Debussy, Sonata for Flute, Viola, Harp * Dylan Thomas, If I Were Tickled * Art Garfunkel, Jimmy Webb, All I Know * Art Garfunkel, Perfect Moment * Two Sleepy People * Some Enchanted Evening * The Promise *

Barbara Allen * Kathy's Song * Waters of March
* **Art Garfunkel, James Taylor,** Crying in the
Rain * **Stephen Bishop,** The Day You Fall in
Love with Me * Losing Myself in You * Madge *
City Girl

*

I am moved to speak of Janice Zwail, the colonics
queen. A Chelsea chick, she cleans your colon
for cash or check. Something clicks for me in our
Queens connection. After the evacuation, behind
the bathroom door, I mention the clickety sound
of colonics, so she tap dances on the hardwood
floor.

—To not get all jummed up, she says, eat kale
and chard and green such things.

Behind the movement, the bard in the mind
goes back to both Flushings.

*

Today I met with my publicist. He wants me
to tweet and to meet my audience where it's
at. ("You love your new record, don't you? You
want 'em to know it exists?") Couldn't I be a
glifter first? Or better, a dripster (see the pen
dwip)? Feel the self-image take a serious hit. Does
nothing embarrass? If I'm to be a tweeter now
then cut a hole in the seat of my trousers; give
me feathered tail. All is fashion. Shame for sale.

O techno-America, tattooed and gadgety, when
do we call you a national twagedy?

*

Today I stopped at the jeweler's shop.
   Does the brilliance belong to the diamond or to
the halogen light?
   Is it the million rods and cones of the
shopper's sight?
   It is the lover's right to capture the movie and
be the bright star of my life.

*

Ah, the flower man. He deals specifically with
   love.
Valentine's is coming up; the business of
   affection will bloom.

Peter runs the Windsor flower shop. I tried to
   find out
if he could tell from the notes he's asked to
   write:
Is it just flowers to sell?
Or does he sometimes run into true love—real
   love,
golden, deep, and mature—two lovers being
   their finest selves?
Does Peter know when the hearts are pure?

No, he says. Love goes on behind a closed
   door.
It's not so easily understood. The lover turns
   buyer
when the night before was good.

                              *

pointillistic age . . . no lateral bond . . .
discrete dots with histories live side
by side . . . intensity more vivid, the picture
   loses truth.
I watched the record become the CD.
I saw in the mix the bass, the percussion,
so readable, so "placed" . . . gone the gestalt
I hardly know my neighbors in the co-op,
there's only eight of them and me . . .
connective tissue . . .

—The trouble with pot, said a doctor I know,
is: the insights, the color, quite wonderful—
are like fireworks . . . there and gone . . .
points in time . . . last year's clouds

Let today sweep away the curriculum—
flatten the structure from Bach to Bill Evans.
Like 21st-century nitrogen-fixing bacteria,
let us all turn to mulch for the new shoots to
   grow.

Arthurs, Senior and Junior, 1999

XI

I wanna be the Big Reveal,
left behind the glory train,
down at the station,
dressed like Arthur,
not the type to win.
The car pulls away,
and there on the platform,
staring at hype and spin—
the authentic artist,
devoted for life,
tools in his head, bemused.
Sleeve full of heart,
a man apart from people,
a freak of another nature,
lost in LOLs and to whom it spells,
lost in thought,
left in the dust of Beethovian bombast,
nonplussed.

I take the world for what it really is.
This that we swim in's not it.
It's the love you make, it's here and gone,
it's a ball in space rotating daily
in an oval path that takes a year.

It's your own rosy-fingered dawn, home base,
it's hidden wrath and petty fear.
It's all the groping printed here.
Words can't cut it. Only the gut can take
    it in.
(What is the name for the smell of the neck
of a newborn, or the word for the touch of
    its skin?)

I am immersed in a world that keeps saying:
O my God. The culture calls and I am a
    wafer
dissolved in it. Only evaporation of the
    present
generation can reveal the Arthurian distillate.

*

IS IT ONLY ME OR DO WE ALL FEEL SCHIZOPHRENIC?
KALEIDOSCOPIC IDENTITIES. LIVING IN FRAGMENTS
EVERY DAY. ACCEPT MULTIPLICITY. CALL IT A
VIRTUE. POETIC—PROSAIC. I AM A MOSAIC. NOW
LET 'EM ALL HAVE THEIR SAY:

MEN

We want to impress, imprint, impregnate. We
wander around wanting to make our marks. (Sing
it good; move their hearts.) We long for love, our
highest value—real love, gorgeous and true, bloody
and sincere. We're not really beasties. Men like

me don't like our hairy chests (and hate a hairy
back). When we're fit to be tied, we huff and
puff and blow the house down. But with children
around, this is excruciating for us.

What we like is sly power. We like to be
alone in a limo in blue jeans and a T-shirt, a
thin cotton one that smells of the bedroom. Our
hips are narrow, we're skinny, and it's after the
show; we're full of the potency of just having
used our "stuff" and made hundreds of thousands
of people high.

But mostly we long for real love. Just like you
do. When we speak truthfully and you respond
with verbal sleight-of-hand, the insincerity breaks
our heart. We move on in our most serious
longing. Through decades we slowly observe what
we're doing here on earth. We go through parts
and try to feel it as a whole—What am I?

*

I was in Venice.
I was alone—
    stalking beauty by the Bridge of Sighs.
Suddenly the object of my eye comes to me
    across the Square to the shade
    of this columned arcade and takes me
    to his table.
And as we walk we are akin.
    —You met me once . . .
I am taken in.

*

My occupation, singing in concert halls, is put aside. I do a piece of movie acting, and walk the southern part of Italy in May 2008.

Now in June, Arthur Junior is my preoccupation. Upstairs all days, I review his life, recorded on my Handycam, on forty-four two-hour videotapes from 1990 to today. Religiously, I cherish his beauty and his beautiful development. Down in the kitchen, the living Arthur Junior emerges . . .

What is to be said between father and son beyond: "Watch me, Dad," and "I love you, son"? Tack to these winds, let all others be bluster. Faith is a goddess; mine is to trust her.

*

I AM DEVOTED TO*:

My WOMAN   A twenty-one-year love affair
   with Kathryn
Raising James Arthur and Beau
My Body of Work—Music   c. 1,000 solo
   concerts; 11 albums (with songs #138
   through #151) just completed
My healthy body

* Written in 2006

MY PEOPLE   Sandy Greenberg; brothers Jules, Jerome; my wife's mother, Patricia Hagen; Jack Nicholson; Jimmy Webb; Paul Simon; Paul Krause; Nicole Hambro

MY BOOKLIST—LITERATURE   Currently reading #1,217, 48 years, 361,980+ pages read, 20.6 pages per day [5/15]

MY EUROWALK   From Shannon, Ireland, in 1998, now 20 legs to 40 kms east of Rome (USA was 40 legs, c. '85–'96)

MY WRITING   May 2015, I am at page 676, entry no. 1,115 in the eighth notebook

FAMILY VIDEOTAPE   Handycam, Super 8, two-hour videos: started 1990, James's baby shower; now shooting #42

DIARY/NOTEBOOK   2½" x 4" day-to-day engagements; '72–today

PHOTOGALLERY (STAIRWAY)   123 framed pictures of my family

JAMES QUOTES BOOK   Page 42, entry no. 227

DIMES   12,840

THE PHILADELPHIA PHILLIES   From Robin Roberts—to help me remember how to not be too happy

*

Why couldn't I be a goldsmith? I could build an entire battle scene in little strips of filigree with separate strands of gold in the horses' manes and set it all on a pinky ring for Kim's

adornment . . . and not have to sing these
nuances, inviting angels onto the head of a pin.

*

SIMON AND GARFUNKEL   *Watched pot, pitted kettle*

*

HAVING WALKED ACROSS THE USA FROM THE MID-'80S
TO THE MID-'90S, I BEGAN TO WALK EUROPE IN 1998:
FROM THE SHANNON AIRPORT IN WESTERN IRELAND
THROUGH A CHAIN-LINK FENCE, ACROSS THE COUNTRY
TO THE SOUTHEAST CORNER. THEN FERRY TO PEMBROKE
IN SOUTHWESTERNMOST WALES, ACROSS ITS SOUTHERN
COAST TO BRISTOL IN ENGLAND. I THEN WENT SOUTH, SAW
SOME OF WEST ENGLAND, AND FERRIED FROM POOLE
TO CHERBOURG, THEN NORMANDY, PARIS, BURGUNDY,
LYON, GRENOBLE, OVER THE ALPS TO ITALY'S PIEDMONT,
AND DOWN TO GENOA, TUSCANY, SIENA, ROME, THEN
NAPLES. NOW ACROSS SOUTHERN ITALY TO BARI, WHERE I
STALLED. (DO I NEED TO SEE GREECE?)

It's fitting that I should return to the road
and finish my voyage to Istanbul. But is it
worth my time to fulfill the dream, to execute
the concept? Is it about Ulysses anymore? Or
a Turkish destination, a Middle East door to the
Syrian war? All the Greece that's east before
me—lambs and white rock, Thessaloniki, the
Bosporus, Troy—tax the sciatica, change at the

Aegean from Iliad boy to the shining Achilles.
From Ireland to the heel of Italy, true to the
original deal. Is there *areté* in Avraham?
  Or am I Don Quixote alone before the
windmills come, with a thousand more kilometers
to Byzantium?

*

I'm up there IN the etchings on the walls
of fine hotels in that other air of Baudelaire
where ice is blue and creviced walls with
frozen waterfalls and stone so steep even
Louis Philippe bows his head in prayer.
He lingers on his way to sleep. Brahms is
not "Romantic" yet. He longs to get away
from care and stare at timeless rock up there.

*

From February 2006 to January 2011 I read
160 books. These 26 books stand out:

Doris Kearns Goodwin, *Team of Rivals* (2005)
Geoff Emerick, *Here, There and Everywhere*
  (2006)
J. P. Donleavy, *The Ginger Man* (1955)
Jonathan Franzen, *The Corrections* (2001)
Isaiah Berlin, *Russian Thinkers* (1978)
Ian McEwan, *On Chesil Beach* (2007)
Jonathan Lethem, *Motherless Brooklyn* (1999)

José Saramago, *The Gospel According to Jesus Christ* (1994)

Reinhold Niebuhr, *Leaves from the Notebook of a Tamed Cynic* (1930)

Booth Tarkington, *The Magnificent Ambersons* (1918)

Evelyn Waugh, *A Handful of Dust* (1934)

D. H. Lawrence, *Lady Chatterley's Lover* (1928)

Henri Troyat, *Tolstoy* (1965)

Fareed Zakaria, *The Post-American World* (2009)

Lao Tzu, *Hua Hu Ching* (c. 6th century BC)

Daniel Defoe, *Roxana* (1724)

Ivan Goncharov, *Oblomov* (1859)

Akira Iriye, *The Origins of the Second World War in Asia and the Pacific* (1987)

Christopher Caldwell, *Reflections on the Revolution in Europe: Immigration, Islam and the West* (2009)

Richard Wright, *Native Son* (1940)

Wilkie Collins, *The Woman in White* (1860)

Kathryn Stockett, *The Help* (2009)

Doug Glanville, *The Game from Where I Stand* (2010)

Jim Harrison, *Legends of the Fall* (1978)

Nassim Nicholas Taleb, *The Black Swan* (2007)

Thomas Wolfe, *Of Time and the River* (1935)

*

MOVING INTO A SECOND SIMON AND GARFUNKEL *OLD FRIENDS* TOUR, JUNE 2009.

My wife came up with a notion:

—How right your voice would be on "Born at
the Right Time," a song from the heart of Paul's
solo career. Now we are engaged in making a
set list for a Simon and Garfunkel tour of the
Far East. Our individual work is included—subsets
within our show.

"Love begets love," I heard in Kathryn's
comment. To play in Otherman's turf is a
generous turn that brings the Divine into play, it
shades the light of the harmonies. Relaxation sets
in. We practice. His song becomes ours. We move
to "For Emily," my solo, a new middle eight is
divined on guitar (from whither?).

—He's illuminating you, she says to me.

The Muse bit the ass of my beautiful wife, and
I had an ear for the insight. A spiral of trust
climbing in colored light. Love makes the Slinky
rise.

*

The windy thing about fathering is having to
    do "The Groucho."
When my son is released from his playpen
    onto the New York sidewalk, his little feet
        pump in sprint time.
Winded, I run with him and the jumping
    blood.
I run with my head as near as can be to his.
    I want the vibrational joy.

Right response is rest. My x and y axes are
    put to a test:
I must run to keep up,
    and do the long-strided sweep of "The
      Groucho" to get down.

*

A friend of mine, Dr. Rony Shimony, goes to a
dentist named Gardenschwartz. A Garfunkel has
to sometimes ask himself, "What's in a name?" Why
does Beryl Sprinkel go into government? Why

Early reunion with Paul Simon. "He's illuminating you,"
Kathryn says. c. 1976

docs Barack Obama? What's with Kelly Tripucka,
the basketball star? The Ayatollah and the
Bogwan Shree Rajneesh may be totally cool, but
Lee Iacocca and Oksana Baiul? An' Netanyahu—
who's kiddin' who? Arthur Streeb-Greebling goes
to Dr. Penbendish; Dr. Haldanish sees Boutros
Boutros-Ghali. Who's the irate Iranian who, each
time he fails to pack it, says: "Ach, . . . my dinna'
jacket"? I know of two women, last names Urdang
and Zwail. Both work in colonics . . . on Joey
Buttafuoco. Something's being said here.

*

Tired of reading Macaulay's *England*,
   I followed the air at sundown.

The older I get, the more it's about the
     air . . .
   how extremely divine the Tahitian air,
   as I stare at the darkening cove.

I must share my appreciation.

   —Are you from here? I grope in English
to the Polynesian girl cleaning my room at the
     tub.

   —No, not here—from Raiatea,
she answers guardedly. She seems twenty-two.

   —I know it. I say and pronounce it back to
     her.

Then I act out how beautiful the air feels to
      me here.
  . . . and so she smiles bashfully,
   dropping her head into the towels
    she holds at her bosom.

Where have I seen this feminine grace,
   this supreme law of serene acceptance in a
    face?

In the paintings of Gauguin!
   (a man with an indigo muse)
The blues drew Paul into the South Pacific,
   but this is what held him the rest of his life.

*

TOGETHER WE THROW OUR BEAU INTO BED, WE SWING
HIM HANDS AND FEET, KIM AND I; AND SING HIM TO
SLEEP:
       Hoist and tickie, hoist and fly

*

"It's always the same zebra,
   we just get to see it from all the angles,"
I said about life some years ago,
   "the eight-year-old angle,
    the twenty-six, the sixty-five."

Now I see the shape of it,
   ways of behavior,

the smell of what's relevant,
animal stripes from flank to mane—

But who can explain the embrace
of the deceased
as the soul revolves to face the beast?

Arthur Jr.'s inner joy

XII

NOW THAT MANY MAY EXPECT TO LIVE
A GENERATION BEYOND AGE 65,
WHAT ARE THESE EXTRA YEARS ABOUT?

a) Devotion to raising Arthur Jr and Beau with Kim
b) Giving. Compassion. Global awareness.
c) Maximize my reputation as one of the world's truly good singers
d) Travel: India, China, Tanzania, Nepal, Dubai, Greenland, the ocean floor
e) Write my autobiography
f) Create a fabulous lair of a second home in the Alps
g) Poll for sociological insight
h) Movie work—hang out in L.A.
i) Enjoy my friends; fall in with a new crowd
j) Develop a new skill—speak Chinese. scout for baseball talent
k) Rabelaisian pleasure-seeking
l) Defy cynicism in government—serve it with honor
m) Amass millions, S&G tour
n) Be a better Buddhist—do all I do now with increased *ichinen*. If it's all in the eye of the beholder, then enrichen the beholder.

*

How to remember de rock 'n' roll of de early days. It was so long ago. We didn't know . . . how could we have but known what would develop? Who knew? We were shadows of our future selves. Fresh from de monaural, we thought stereo was big. We had melody, chord changes, grooves, we didn't know you could sing de song a little bit and machines would make it so beautiful. Who knew, in dos early days, you could drop de melodies and de chords and just bark out de words, angry-style? We thought we were hip—we didn't know about de hip and de hop an' de hype. We balanced our sounds in dos days—who knew you could boost de bass and shake de room? We didn't know de tunes could be so piercing in de treble. We didn't have digital. We didn't pierce anything. People's skin was so empty. Nobody knew to put ball bearings in de eyebrow and in de nose. We were dumb. It was analogue. We didn't even know you could put blue and red pictures on ya neck. Fe life. In dos days we just had Elvis an' de Fab Four. We didn't have vowels before our things—der were no iPads, emails, no e-tunes. FAX were tings ya knew. You couldn't Google, you couldn't tweet a song. You couldn't steal a copyright yet. We didn't know how to break de heart of rock 'n' roll. It was de Dark Ages.

*

   —Life is for enjoyment.
This is what eighty-year-old Mabel Morris
      said to me
at a nursing home in Hollywood forty years
      ago.
I was taping her for *Bookends*. (She wore a
      pin
that read "MGM.") But I say, now that I'm
      nearer
the other end,
   —Life is to spend; we give it up for . . .
      something.

These days I sing "Bridge Over Troubled
      Water"
for a full arena with fear of hernia. My mind
      is torn
between mortal and might—do I hold the
      finale
in check? I feel a tear to the right of my gut,
but it hasn't torn yet . . .

So I give them my heart, my strength, my
      spleen.
I span that bridge from town to town and
      give away
what might have been to spend what's left of
      the
life within.

*

I don't think of cake when I think about
     birthdays—
   every year a candle in the grand
     candelabrum.
I think of a blade, with every swing
     descending through
   the years—everything nears the pendulum.

AUGUST 11, 2008

*

Who will speak at whose funeral? When I said,
"You'll outlast me, you live more carefully," he
said, "Write out what you want." Okay . . . it's
hard to say I knew Artie well, he was enigmatic
to himself.

   Which of us was more aware? Which the elder?
I was born November 5—he on October 13, a few
weeks premature. Were we both conceived at the
same instant—February 5, 1941, the dead middle of
winter in the heart of World War II? Was I born
at the right time?

   For two-thirds of a century his arm has been
around my shoulder. He's dazzled me with gifts.
I nurtured him in his youth. He brought me into
prominence. I taught him to sing. He connected
my voice to the world. I made us stand tall. All
of our personal belongings are intertwined.

We say it's exhausting to compete but we
shine for each other. It's still our favorite game.
It goes on, this embrace, whether I speak for him
or he for me. Love ruled our lives. It rules the
mourners, and the winner of longevity.

SIMON VS. GARFUNKEL

X

Nam myoho renge kyo Baruch atah Adonoi
Elohenu Melech haolam: Blessed art Thou, my
God, King of the Universe—I give you my
awareness and my appreciation for sustaining
my life throughout and bringing me alive to
this point. Be with me again today, throughout
the day, ever-present. Help me, guide me to
be a better man—one who is aware, as much
as possible, of the hurt I cause others, of the
sharpness and power of my tongue. Extend, O
God, my ability to see the fool I am, the harm
I do, and all my great limitations. Today I want
to walk a more humble path, to love You and all
Your manifestations on earth. I need You to carry
on in decency. Let me respect my simple self as
a statement of beautiful life, but help me not be
"proud," nor preen my feathers, nor to find any
human being as less than me, for this is to judge.
And You are the judge and giver of all life.
Connect me, dear Lord, to my earliest days when
I knew my relationship to You and sang to You

with prayer. Today I pray to find that line again
and serve Your way.

Help me, find me again in my lost state today,
with all my "wisdom" and separation. Let me see
my true helpers—my wife, my sons, my friends—
as your gifts to me. Shepherd me again as in
days before I was five feet. Pull me back, please
God, from my sharp-pointedness just before—
not after—I cut another with acute "accuracy"
and cause pain to others, for all of them are
Yours. I do love this world with an immensity
that is bound within it. My remorse, my sins, are
crushing but I will not be crushed. With Your
guidance, please God, from this moment on, I will
seek to extend my goodness and I will see signs
around me that You wish it.

*

MID-TOUR, NAGOYA, JAPAN. July 8, 2009. This is
the fifth season. Beyond discontent. This is what
is meant by bewitchment. The end of wonder.
Heart-springs spent in a winter down under.

*

In the arena the echo's extreme,
the sounds sing twice as they fall.

Writers tend to win: well-timed jokes take all.
At the sound check, this from Paul:

"You know the joke of the big vagina?"
(I'm the bounce, he has the ball)

A woman with one goes to her doctor,
All depressed, she tries to stall.

—Open wide, he says with maximum gall.
You have a big vagina.

You have a big vagina.
—You don't have to tell me twice, she tells him.
—I didn't, he says.

Reverberant laughter rafter to wall
Fertility fills the hall.

*

This is the season of victory
Sushi returns from sashimi
Time and reason are done with me
The runner can walk again.

Whole nations have been impregnated,
Gone is the time to be seen.
Now I can see. The screen is black.
I belong to the back of the balcony,
To the tree of expanded vitality runny with
    song.

*

WHAT IT WAS:
VIDEO * 1) OLD FRIENDS * 2) A HAZY SHADE
OF WINTER * 3) I AM A ROCK * 4) AMERICA
* 5) KATHY'S SONG * 6) HEY, SCHOOLGIRL *
7) BE-BOP-A-LULA * 8) SCARBOROUGH FAIR
* 9) HOMEWARD BOUND * VIDEO * 10) MRS.
ROBINSON * 11) SLIP SLIDIN' AWAY * 12) EL
CONDOR PASA * 13) BRIGHT EYES * 14) A HEART
IN NEW YORK * 15) PERFECT MOMENT * 16) NOW
I LAY ME DOWN TO SLEEP * 17) BOY IN THE
BUBBLE * 18) ME AND JULIO * 19) DIAMONDS
ON THE SOLES OF HER SHOES * 20) THE ONLY
LIVING BOY IN NEW YORK * 21) MY LITTLE
TOWN * 22) BRIDGE OVER TROUBLED WATER *
23) THE SOUND OF SILENCE * 24) THE BOXER *
25) LEAVES THAT ARE GREEN * 26) CECILIA

*

When do-si-dos are over, show the hidden
heart—honor your partner.

*

AUGUST 2009. ALL IS WELL RIGHT NOW. I FALL
ASLEEP WHEN I HIT THE PILLOW. I CARRY NO
DEBTS. MOTHER AND JULES ARE GONE FROM HERE.
DAD IS LONGER GONE. I HAVE GIVEN JEROME
A "SAFETY NET" FROM FINANCIAL DISTRESS. HE
AND CINDY ARE MARRYING NEXT MONTH. BEAU IS
DEEPLY SECURE, I BELIEVE, HAPPY AND PLAYFUL.

KATHRYN AND I ARE DEEPER IN LOVE. SHE CAPTIVATES ME AND WINS MY RESPECT THROUGH THE YEARS. WINNING A TONY THIS YEAR IS A VALID OPTION FOR MY GIFTED ROOMMATE, LOVER, MOTHER OF BEAU AND ARTHUR JUNIOR—*the bildungsroman*—JULIEN SOREL. MY OWN WORK PROSPECTS HAVE BIG S&G SHOWS, MAYBE IN 2018. THE CAT IS ALWAYS FINE. THANK GOD MY HEALTH IS GOOD. THE PHILLIES ARE IN FIRST AND MAY NOW WIN A SECOND WORLD SERIES IN A ROW.

*

Aristotle has always been dry to me.

Vico's *New Science* 1720s look at developing Western consciousness from earliest Man through the Greek Golden Age is insightful.

Out of the bathroom comes Beau.

—No, two Hershey kisses, Mommy. Two? I made pee pee *and* poo poo.

*

Managua, Nicaragua we go rollin' along

One day I take my son to Nicaragua. Mr. Gomez has called the William Morris Agency and booked me to sing at his home in Managua—sixtieth birthday, hundred guests poolside. My boy came for the life experience, to extend his good fortune, to further impregnate the gods. The

James Arthur Garfunkel, age sixteen, on a
motorcycle trip in the South of France

boys and I did the show we do. Junior sang "The
Very Thought of You," then stayed beyond my
departure with the host.

Now he and Gomez go rolling along to a place
where cigars are made. Over lunch, when they
ask him to sing, he gets up and launches into

—Smile, though your heart is aching
 Smile, even though it's breaking . . .

and brings two hundred women to a hush. He is a
harbinger of universal laws. In a factory shack in
Managua, Nicaragua, rolling takes a pause.

*

SHORTLY AFTER THIS I LOST MY VOICE.

*

Love worms its way into the interstices. It plays
with the stitching at the seams. The edge of
a satin blanket on the baby's upper lip. Asleep
facedown, I bring my cheek to the corner of the
pillow for the cozy. My baby calls me "Ovie,"
sounds like oven. It used to be "doll of dolls," in
time it changed to "of." Yes, Love brings all pomp
to defeat. I call her sweeter than sweet.

*

Now I'm in the warp and weave of alive, there
is no plan no next as known, I'm on my own; the
tour is off the voice still mending the money
is all given back. I will take my Kathryn to St.
Tropez and look at her. Maybe we'll look at the
Mediterranean Sea and see white and blue—at
three on the terrace a robin's egg shade, air
blue, may surround her; at six in the morning
opalescent ivory looks out from my calendar.

*

JUNE 2010

What is the singing voice to me?
A name, a skill, or a flag I see? A certain
thrill—the gift of glide, the ride on the
cusp of emotion, uplift from the heart
to the cords, love for the song, for the
sound . . . FOR 4 MONTHS, THE GIFT IS GONE.

*

Somewhere past the middle of the '60s, I took
a room at the Hampshire House. I remember the
carpet—cherry vermilion. A balcony looked up
the axis of Central Park. Dead center, 25th floor.
I was new to fame and to room service. It must
have been spring. I smelled it at the terrace—
standing there in my underwear, toes in the
rug, drinking freshly squeezed. Equidistant from
Central Park West and Fifth Avenue, the world
was mine, I was a rock. The air was kissed. I was
the *arrivist*.

More chart success and real marriage have
brought me here to my family while I fight
for my voice to return. Forty-four years have
passed. They still like my friend and me. Our
"Old Friends" show, our scarcity, have made us,
perhaps, the hottest tour on earth. The world
awaits for two one-inch cords to mend and
return to symmetry—the pinnacle of purpose
prepared for me.

Yesterday my five-year-old son went to his classmate's birthday party. The magician, Domino, did his show. The act was lame. My boy said, "I saw the penny drop," and gave the trick away. The mom who booked him felt cheated. Moments of "ta-dah" fell flat with the kids three times in a row. Poor Domino.

If you play for the crowd, you're subject to whim. Fate makes a foolish object of him whose magic turns tragically gradually grim.

*

gnarly tree
   surrounding me
twisted limbs are gnashed
   and bent above
offshoots from the trunk of many years
the hidden "g" in what appears
   to be my funk and fears
      dancing in the branches

attorney's notes, the need to sing,
gone is everything that palliates;
rip-off rates, my soul invested
   and everywhere I turn
      domestic concern nested
         in a tree house

      under a bower
         beneath all this
            and in the shade of it

my love holds me in her kiss
hyacinth exhalations
 from her baby's breath
  and bare neck and shoulders
 wrap around me in comfort-
soothing, steady, honeysuckle comfort
gnats above can't touch us

This is my Kathryn.
 Under my arm
a garland of beauty
 charm of the arbor
  my darling
   my harvest
    my karma

      *

Soon I will die
 And so soon will we all, my friends;
Important lives will end.

With what?
 The Big Bang? A whimper? A tribute?
 A summation? Tears? Reckoning?
 Anyone noticing? Reassessment? Rest?
 A fallen leaf blown through the grass?

So much for matter. But there at the
 teeniest molecular level, science can't
 decide if the building block of all

matter *is* matter, or is it a wave?
A disturbance. A cause to move.

Didn't I do that? Didn't I make my
    contribution to the collective vibe?
    On the plane of spirit/energy (the
    invisible no-stuff stuff) I worked
    in sound and moved the waves my way.
    People received me warmly. The heat
    sustains me. The earth may take me.

I will write in smoke from my slow-burning
    leaf.

The hidden "g" in benign

XIII

My partner is Sancho Panza.
He picks me up when the sun goes down.
We sleep in towns with two-star inns,
And travel to Macedonia.

My cousin conquered the fields of Spain
Four hundred years ago.
His mind in a majesty
Vision as clear as Vincent van Gogh's.

Kathryn is my Dulcinea
Thessaloniki the prize
Eyes that see archaeology
Are wet with windmill pictures.

I slay them all with song in my throat
I am Don Quixote.

GREECE, WEST OF METSOVO

Yesterday I went to see *The Social Network*.
There was the star, a heartless Harvard wallflower
cashiering the privacy of everyone's face he could
get his computer around. Bypassing the moral
issue, he and his "friends" feasted on the roasting

of individuals (feeling human beings, a half a million wieners on a grill for worldwide consumption . . . as if privacy, civility, taste, and discretion had given way to speedy, cerebral cleverness). Power to the People taken from the individual. He learned the game from music downloaders—the taking of individual achievements (special things) and making it people-owned stuff.

One of my vocal cords has gone dysfunctional since February 2010. I can't find the desire to go into the recording studio and try for another special thing. It has become water from a faucet—a thingless stream. My heart is in protest. I cannot render to these new people that which is God's.

*

I played the Tokyo Dome last year with Paul. We sold out the 48,000-seat baseball stadium twice so quickly we added a third—the Budokan, 9,000 seats. If Simon had played the dome alone, would he make a million yen? He *is* a big name, but *is* the duo eight times bigger or ten? How to conceive of a ten-to-one ratio: turn the pages from the start of the dictionary, stop at 90 percent in—you get *toothpick*. You can Twist Unjust Verbosity With Xenon Yielding Zoon; but everything from *a* to *t* allows a greater tune.

*

The fog has lifted for me. I see my true self-worth. My Simon and Garfunkel body of work is an achievement of great beauty. It needs nothing with it to stand tall. Not Paul Revere, Paul McCartney, or Paul Gauguin. The Beatles stand alone. As does S&G. An imaginary painter, Johan van Jeers, would love to combine his work with Rembrandt's, and sell the Dutch couple. How does Rembrandt feel about this?

*

WHEN I LEARNED THAT A CONTRACT HAS BEEN PREPARED FOR ME TO SIGN WITH SONY, AUTHORIZING THEM TO RELEASE AN ALBUM COUPLING SIMON AND GARFUNKEL WITH PAUL SIMON, I WENT TO SWITZERLAND.

OCTOBER 2010

*

The Brienzersee is next to me where litigants
    have died.
Songs are sung on the Thunersee, west on
    the other side.
Between, I am in Interlaken rock 'n' roll has
    done me wrong.
Split my soul, stopped my song.

*

From February 2011 to January 2015 I read 89 books. These 24 books stand out:

John Muir, *A Thousand-Mile Walk to the Gulf* (1867)
Michael Soussan, *Backstabbing for Beginners* (2008)
Elie Wiesel, *Night* (1958)
Luigi Pirandello, *One, No One & One Hundred Thousand* (1909–26)
Niobe Way, *Deep Secrets* (2011)
Albert Goldman and Lawrence Schiller, *Ladies and Gentlemen—LENNY BRUCE!!* (1971)
Henry Kissinger, *On China* (2011)
J. W. von Goethe, *The Man of Fifty* (1818)
Sanford D. Greenberg, *Even This We Will Be Pleased to Remember* (2011)
Michael Shaara, *The Killer Angels* (1974)
Mario Puzo, *The Fortunate Pilgrim* (1964)
E. L. James, *Fifty Shades of Grey* (2011)
Nancy Mitford, *Voltaire in Love* (1957)
Margaret MacMillan, *The War That Ended Peace: The Road to 1914* (2013)
James Fenimore Cooper, *The Deerslayer* (1841)
Victoria Wilson, *A Life of Barbara Stanwyck* (2013)
Hugh Trevor-Roper, *History and the Enlightenment* (2010)
Erik Larson, *In the Garden of Beasts* (2011)
Don DeLillo, *Cosmopolis* (2003)
Sinclair Lewis, *Main Street* (1920)
William Manchester, *Winston Spencer Churchill: The Last Lion, Part 2: Alone 1932–1940* (1988)

Robert D. Kaplan, *The Revenge of Geography*
(2012)
George Eliot, *Felix Holt: The Radical* (1866)
Alice Munro, *Dear Life* (2012)

*

O Jungfrau out my window,
Eiger round the way,
The falcon cannot hear me,
Witness my dismay:

Out on the balcony,
    here at the peak of the continent,
War and Peace are tearing at my core—
The glory of my music life
    is up for grabs and bargained for.

Was I just a pawn in someone else's game?
Midwife or The Man? Someone's song?
    or Singer, with an insight of his own?
Set to soar, but made to play along?

Poet or prosaic,
Prometheus bound or in flight?
Mercury ascending or bloody Mars in a fight?

INTERLAKEN, SWITZERLAND
OCTOBER 28, 2010

*

Autumn in the Alps . . . eleven-o-seven, a
radiant morning. I walk toward the Jungfrau, to
the town of Allmend. Breathe out.

Going on sixty-nine next week, but first—
Halloween. Let the deepest sigh of the mind,
of the spleen, and the heart between say
"Aahhhh . . ." My natural day goes this way:
Herald Tribune and coffee still, *toward* but never
reaching Understanding . . . the pen finds the
paper, it is noon when I begin. Here on earth
there is never Understanding, only the specific—
two men are carrying a load of broken branches
in an olive-brown six-by-eight hammock-thing. The
lungs inflate. The heart can't help but love. (We
never chose our nose or to live.)

Look up from here—

O hear my song O God of all the nations. A song of peace for their land and mine.

Itinerant minstrel, mute with awe—offer the
rare and the raw. Render unto God what is
His. . . . How do you do it, lordalmighty! How did
you put those rocks up there? I must give praise
for every inch, for sunlit days like these when
perception of your magnificent construction is a
cinch . . . ignore the fan letter, Lord, you're busy,
I'll just lay it at your feet. It's all I can do to
add depth to my life. It's Bach's and my conceit.
My woman, my children, and You who dropped

the snow. Glistening tracks are in it. . . . My
faith is my lifelong construction . . . the cedars,
the straw bales, the strawman, the cowbells, the
melting, the melting—all that is, allmending. I turn
to go.

*

Rhythm and rock are fixed. It's my perception
of the cliff that shifts. There, the spilling crevice
of my early college years, I was Rousseau,
le savoyard. There they spill still. Forty-eight
years have passed since those Vespa-riding days.
("*J'entends siffler le train*.") There was gunmetal
gray in the mountain face. World War II was over.
   Wood burns after the summer's end. A ten-
year-old looks up at me at the cable-car window,
thrilled by the Alps and the spill. He wants to
know if I enthuse. The Grand Chiseler still speaks
to me now, the grays have purples and blues.
   I hear. Or not, I muse.

*

  10 years old is a whip—one skater pulls
    another along. You're ten.
  20 was in the tunnel of inner ferment, mostly
    unnoticed.
  30 was a cricket on your shoulder, from the
    swampland, marking time.
  40 was a goad. Do it now. Swim hard.

50s not so nice. Like a scotch 'n' soda—a
face-off with The Big Man.
60 starts denial for real—mind control—poetic
surrealism.
70 is the worst of the seven. It's got badness
all seeped into it—no more trees, no breeze,
no this.
80 you don't wanna know. And yet you do.
Take me there, O Lord.
At 90 it all makes sense. You're out of your
own way. In love.

*

Circumcision—where's the rub? Pleasure-robbing
hospital habit. It's not that the thrill is gone, just
somewhat taken away. Come men, be indignant.
We need orgasm accounts from those without
and those guys with, all over the world. (Hold
the *mohel* with the paring knife there—we must
compare levels of ecstasy.) And what about the
trauma to the child? Don't we know, in the 21st
century: All is imprinted from birth somewhere—
    O tender infant, infinitely divine, must we
feel that post-womb life can sting like lightning
between the legs, just out of the blue?

*

**Health is purpose.
Acting toward the goal is a verb.
All, to me, is metaphor.**

Here logs sit in a self-conscious pit,
   all aglow like nouns.

I place new wood atop. The blaze leaps up.
The bed alit is food for the action,
   now consumed in turn.
The verb in the hearth is to burn.

                    WHERE IS MY SINGING VOICE?

                    *

I am an old boatman.
I cast my net of pretense before me.
Then I sail into it.

I dreamed I was packing for David Crosby
   for a flight in two hours. When the clothes
      were in,
I started on the music, all in my kitchen in a
      box.
   He said, "Pack the vinyl, tapes, and CDs
      thoroughly.
Send it all after me." Many dozens, the
      bottom of my drawer
   —it was a major cleaning out.
I awoke to the notion that the clearing wasn't
      for Crosby.
   It was me. A foreshadow of my demise. I
      have cast
my imagination before me. The people at my
      funeral—

diverse associates of mine—they knew an
    Arthur
who hardly knew himself. They grapple with
    identity,
    like the blind feeling a gondolier:

The old camp counselor, the drummer, the
    woman I married.
    "How could we know the same man?" My
    son implores
my partner, "Who was he?" Crosby measures
    Sanford
    speaking to the tunesmith. They all assess
    the deceased.
There at the intersection of all their points
    of view,
    I lie in their hearts.

Sweet Arthur, son of Jack and Rose, brother
    of Jules
    and Jerome, sailing home in my little poem.

*

"Car!" we called in Queens. So we stopped the
game and stepped aside. Now I walk in northern
Greece, from Igoumenitsa to Istanbul. A week
to Thessaloniki. The Greek economy falling
down. Sixty-two years have now gone by. Mount
Olympus up ahead. Apollo may have played in
this very lake where lately Plato had his country
estate. I walk *with* traffic on the right of the road.

Now the game is to listen behind me for the sound of tires, then move to the right and think "Car."

*

Today I lost Duke Snider, my handsome centerfielder. Tonight Jane Russell died. He was eighty-four. She was a screen star in '54, with Marilyn. I was the horny adolescent, sitting in the back row watching them. Main Street movie theater. Winter coat upon my lap. Scared stiff but getting sticky. That's how good the acting was.

Snider and Russell, him and her prototypes. But bigger than the Duke, better than Mantle and Mays, stands the Cardinal, muse of mysterious ways, romance in a newsreel, hunched in a question mark, the great Stan Musial.

*

My lover wants to meet me in the afterlife.
What in the world could this possibly mean?
Is it "I will follow you" gone wild?
(My heart jumps to 100 on the treadmill screen.)
Or is it love gone long and I'm just beguiled?

Wrap me up in endlessness, sign me on for
    dateless death.
Honey hold me in your infinite kiss.
Be my wife outside of time,
In a free fall that feels like this,
Outlasting all known rhythm in our rhyme.

HAUNTED BY THE LOSS OF SINGING, FEBRUARY 3, 2011

*

THIS IS AN ERA OF NEEDLESS FEAR. I SING TO SOOTHE.
LYING ON THE MASSAGE TABLE, I THINK ABOUT THIS:

It's curious to me, I tell the masseur, that
        baseball bats have gone
    from ash to maple, in the pros.
So an infielder not on his toes
    is now up for the pierce and slash of flying
        wooden torpedoes.

Why does the talk-show host sit on a chair
        that's higher than
    the guest? Am I the only one who notices
        this?
The majestic Craig Ferguson and the imperial
        egos of all the rest
    Seem rude to the person they're talking
        to . . . curious.

—Anytime you can smash your opponent in
        the face it motivates
    your team, I heard a sportscaster say.
Is it a kinder, gentler generation or
        what? . . . I'm just curious.

When I see television medicine ads, the dire
        warnings of
    fifteen possible side effects scare me away
        from the product.

Across America concert at Ellis Island, 1997

Is it just me? Am I being tough? Why would
    anyone take this stuff?
    . . . just curious.

And how, exactly, do you abuse a drug?

I don't think I ever heard *Longoria* till Eva,
    the desperate
housewife made it a household name.
Along comes Evan Longoria of the Tampa
    Bay Rays.
    What's the game?

Picnic in Central Park, New York City.
Beau is two years old.

XIV

I'd rather be in Breughel's world,
   four more centuries wise;
Heaven knows why Flemish tableaux
   of the earth are filled with skies.

Here I walk on the road to Aix-en-Provence,
   where the cube was born;
Reality worn away for the man
   who chopped it up, Paul Cézanne.

England had Tudors,
   but the continent's faith was higher;
Ask the Medicis about Palestrina
   or the reach of a Gothic spire.

Give me the dead white old boys' club,
   Johann Bach and the young Jean-Jacques;
Picasso can paint their shoes
   and Salvador Dalí can bend a clock.

David Bowie's a personal pal,
   but Warhol and him? Guess what I say—
Peter the Elder paints landscape art
   to steal the heart away.

*

Let them all go to email. I prefer the page.
I remember when it evoked an earlier age.
Now the madeleine is all the rage.

Poor Proust—an epiphany in his shoe.
Soon Tiffany will sell his silver spoon,
And tea with Swann and me in the afternoon.

I don't need a quill to still be heard.
Imagine a thoughtful word could still get
        through to the textless conversation of
        the few.

Not the guy with the sightless eye on his cell
        phone,
Nor the girl in a BlackBerry world with a
        tone-deaf ear . . . am I the only one
        who's here?

*

I walk in light rain through a square
    in Aix-en-Provence.
My love is like the lime umbrellas of Cherbourg
    and like morning dreams sprung to day,
blown in the secret "h" of a whim,
    the way a nylon dome succumbs to Him,
        it lifts, inverted in a breeze
        —it's Kim!

*

I try to be a wordsmith and send it in the
    mail.
After the salutation, words fail.
I stumble on in frailty. You are the very heart
    of me.
Now I see it was love at first sight.
There in the kitchen, your wide eyes took me
    in.
My soul was akin to yours and to all
   that might be within us.

Twenty-five years have passed.
You stopped time still.
I never pull back from the circle we're in
   to observe with perspective all that has been.

In your vast ocean, my will is a ship.
Even in my dreams I can't get a grip.
You have become my everything—frightening
   for love to be so strong.
With Arthur and Beau as embodiments,
   I can still sing—This is my song.

TO PRECIOUS KATHRYN

*

I found my wife in a crevice in the globe,
   a corner of the Roman Colosseum.

She taught me a new way to fight
and how to write the Book of Job:
display your pain in an open wound museum,
make it personal—bleed with all your might.

*

LIFE ACHIEVEMENTS

#25   Singing the sound track to *The Graduate*,
      1967 film

#24   Acting in *Catch-22*, 1970 film

#23   Producing, singing *Songs from a Parent to
      a Child*, 1997 album

#22   Singing four hours of repertoire as
      cantor at my Bar Mitzvah (1954)

#21   Reading the *Random House Dictionary*,
      1,664 pages, all 275,000 words (1998)

#20   Making *Across America*, a TV special of
      my concert at Ellis Island (1996)

#19   Producing, singing *Watermark*, 1977 album

#18   Finding, designing our New York City
      apartment, 1975

#17   Reading 1,219 books (1969–2015)

#16   Songwriting, singing *Everything Waits to
      Be Noticed*, 2002 trio album

#15   Producing, singing *Parsley, Sage, Rosemary
      and Thyme*, 1966 album

#14   Singing *Old Friends* show, S&G concert
      tours I and II, in USA, Europe, and Far
      East, 2003, 2004, and 2009

#13   Attaining BA and MA degrees from
Columbia College and University
(1958–1967)

#12   Walking across Japan, USA (1984–1996),
and Europe (1998–2014)

#11   Acting in *Bad Timing*, 1980 film

#10   Producing, singing *The Animals'
Christmas*, 1986 album

#9   Writing *Still Water*, 1989 book of prose
poems

#8   Creating the Art Garfunkel concert
(4-man, 1-man band), (1991, 2013) and
touring the world with it

#7   Acting in *Carnal Knowledge*, 1971 film

#6   Producing, singing *Angel Clare*, 1973
album

#5   Producing, singing *Breakaway*, 1975

#4   Performing *The Concert in Central Park*,
September 19, 1981

#3   Producing, singing *Bookends*, 1968 album

#2   Producing, singing *Bridge Over Troubled
Water*, 1970 album

#1   Marrying Kathryn (1988), creating James
(Arthur Jr., 1990) and Beau (2005)

*

**A train with freight. I am the weight and wit
of an angel incarnate.**

*

THE PITTED KETTLE

The resound of a thousand years. Invented in
    Ireland,
Grecian earned, wage of a journeyman—
The road of distress and experience—
The broken cup of kindness I bear for a
    thousand
      thousand strides.

It is my pitted kettle—
A helmet holding every picture of the search
    for
    infinity's resonance,
Dented by the blackbird's peck in a trek of
    speckled radiance.

WALKING NORTHERN GREECE

*

We live in a state of flux. Only in movement
do we recognize life—all things on their
way to being. December 2, 2011. Soon my
son Arthur Junior will be home for the
holidays, but first Beau, his mommy, and I
will go to Florida to visit Kim's mom . . .
my voice continues to mend. It's almost
two years since the end of January 2010,
when it suddenly failed. I don't really know
why . . . months of rest, unison singing to
James Taylor, Chet Baker, the Everlys, and

my own past work. Bring back the tones,
singing in the recording studio, no luck. In
late 2010 I took to the stage with mic and
speakers, to an empty house of a thousand.
Lately I tried to sing three songs to an
audience . . . adrenaline . . . at the Buddhist
Center . . . too fragile. In two days I'll try
another four-song set in Irvington. I accepted
a ninety-minute charity gig for March 2012
in Toronto—five songs, lots of talk. I put
away pot smoking on August 21, 2010,
and began pills and psychiatry. . . . Beau's
in kindergarten, sadness and anger have
appeared in him. Kim is my rock steady love
light. Sex has fallen away. Paul Simon is involved
with himself. Hopes of an S&G tour are on the
back back burner. . . . Sandy Greenberg has
become Chairman of the Board of Governors
of the Johns Hopkins Wilmer Eye Institute. He
wants to cure blindness! He has just given me
his 550-page magnificent life story. He is my
true brother. I read my book #1,152, Niobe
Way's *Deep Secrets.* And I continue walking
southeast across Europe from Ireland to
Istanbul. Jerome and Cindy are in Saugerties
(hardly see him). Matt Craig and I work at
the Cutting Room. We sequence the best
recorded vocals of my life's work—two CDs,
34 songs (nine S&Gs). It is *The Singer.*

*

My son is dreams. His father is clouds rotating
round. Do dreams fertilize the day the way
that clouds discharge the pent-up rain?
Does the fertile plain evaporate and all
concerns arise at night?

*

Pan to the east. Europe in the rear. The
afternoon opens on Here. "A day of dappled
sea-borne clouds," floating fleece, fringed with
gray. Spring in Greece. What a dream to be in—
Adriatic to Aegean. This is that other air! Here,
green fields of flax, down to the Dardanelles. O
Earth—you are too beautiful to tell. Thirteen
years of heartswells.

*

WHO AM I IF I'M NOT A SINGER?

Finally I come to the boiling point—
　　two hundred eleven degrees.
The heat of frustration has brought me here
　　to the crucible, to the eye of the beast
that speaks: "You'll never sing again."

Eat the anguish; get down on the mat.
　　Be a reading chair in your mother's womb,
throw it around the hotel room—
　　eleven times against the walls.
Scream for equilibrium.

Thirty years of rulership have brought
    the Egyptians to just below steam.
When the ruler announces he won't quite
       quit,
    they chew on disbelief.

That night an Arab soldier wrestles with a
       dream
    of the man he longs to be.
Eyelashes rest on the sleeping Egyptian
    and on his burning cheek,
      and on the brave singer, mute for a year
      and a week.

Warriors' blood speaks eloquently,
    so God lifts the temperature one degree.

FEBRUARY 13, 2011

*

I have a styptic pencil. I use it to stanch the
    blood.
Surrounded by no exits where tensions stem
    from all of them,
    I hemorrhage from my underworld, my
    Hades.
Hence the need for styptics. For the river Styx,
    my river of hate, begins to flow.

I'm not a famous angel then; I hardly know
    my name.

Sandy Greenberg, Paul Simon, and Jimmy Webb at my wedding, September 18, 1988

XV

Today was the day I returned to the studio. I declared an end to my personal drought, put doubt in the music business aside, and booked time. I employed a few musicians and paid them very well. Faith in rock 'n' roll.

Robin Gibb recovers from a coma. What brought him back from the edge—his mother, his doctor, the power to pray? I heard they played him pieces of the album he was making at the time he slipped away. Did he say, in the climb from a very deep hole: "I gotta get back to my rock 'n' roll"?

*

All the people around me are elsewhere. Unaware, in their phones. But I work in shades of opalescence. Pinks and blues are tints I use but silver is the essence. Refined, exquisite, timed to the visit of rhyme. Simply tell the story. Teeth and tongue, let the lungs commit to the start of the word. Let the bird in your throat explode in flight. Be there in the millionth of a second. Let the consonant speak, the arrow resound, and the vowel ensue in a quiver of sound.

*

George, the Greek, at the Nectar café: "The
trouble is only in Athens," he says, "policy
is made in the seaport towns. Urns are from
Macedonia. The ones who did the fighting, like
monuments in Little Rock, are honored on
pottery in the Met."

Without a trace of Thrace, the euro holds in
its embrace modern Greece. Here I walk through
empty mountains. Beautiful. Still. Thessaloniki
ahead. The leaves are in their infancy, but the
ways of man are old. The European Union,
the Hanseatic League, the Friars, the Masons,
the Persian War. Sigma Chi in Vietnam.

How many cycles are buried beneath the earth?
Poppies by the roadside. The turn of the tide.
Tabula Rasa. Strata Incognita.

*

The other day I lost my voice it's all okay
I didn't like to sing that much.

I always made contact with the fiercest
of lions because I could sing in the cage.
Now I lost rapport and at my
age I'm in a cage once more. The lions are
always in a rage. It's the business of
performance—no blood, no stage—it's
what they know. Today, one clawed my

toe and took the smallest piece of me.
On Monday we do another show.

*

I see Tom Wolfe. He lives down the end of my
block. White suit and boater—a wonderful
man. His frame is askew now (a lifetime of love
for the pen?). Closer to me are the Golden
Rule establishments: the Steiner School,
grounded in the love of fairness, sitting
side-by-side with the mayor ("he with the
gold rules"). I like this man enormously—he's
dear, he's decent, and seems like a lover of
excellence. I am adjacent. I cultivate naïveté.
I imagine we're all in love. Hearts on fire, the
glory of the Gift makes forms of blasé a pack
of lies. We strive to get to heaven and stay out
of trouble behind our watchful eyes.

*

Can the world live with a nuclear Iran, which,
like Japan, has nuclear power but not weapons,
or am I at the flashpoint near the Strait of
Hormuz in Dubai in the Mall of the Emirates at
the base of a ski slope, changing at the lockers
across from a black-robed woman? She, a Muslim;

I, a Jew, looking at the veiled face and into her eyes for a clue.

*

I'm a thousand times faster than the swiftest
     snail.
I beat a running turtle five hundred to one.
To compare me to the hare, where I would
     trail, is unfair.
I'm not a gazelle; I'm not on the run.

It's only the road to Istanbul
I choose my pace and take my place—
where someone decided a brand-new pope'll
     preside in the East in Constantinople.

*

I don't know sailing, but I know you tack to the wind. The sun is south at one at the end of May. My path is east-northeast. At 11:15, the sun is beside me to guide my way.

The walk is a week to Thessaloniki. I set my invisible sail and track to the sun. Through the day it circles my starboard shoulder. And leaves me cold and lost when clouds roll in.

Oliver's giving my son the cold shoulder. He doesn't want to be his friend anymore. How can I tell him that shade was made for the light? How can I find *my* way in the afternoon?

Together we travel, lured to the aft, warm in
the leeward wing of the craft.

*

MAYBE 2010'S THE YEAR OF
GIVING IT UP.

I started it with the end of singing in the
    beginning
of the year. Then Philip Roth stopped writing.

Tony La Russa, his managing days are
    through.
Singing, writing, and baseball too—
what are the three of us gonna do?

But do you ever really stop the thing you
    love?

If Philip had insomnia and inspiration struck,
would he really turn on the television?

When Tony's at his grandson's game and asked
to give advice, won't he contribute without
thinking twice?

See Arthur in that hospital—he steals away
to that stairwell there, and returns to "The
    Lord's Prayer."

*

I don't have to sing no more no more. I'm crushed and broken. Who cares? No one wants to deal with me. I tangle with all their confusion and end up displaying how ugly man can be, to my lover and my seven-year-old. I can't escape the Big Reveal—I am painfully flawed. I live in heartbreak hotel.

*

ROAD MAP

1. Root your faith. Deeply. Firmly. Use family.
2. Challenge everything. Fame is value plus spin, or just spin (bandwagonism).
3. Pleasure: deep (four-year vocal recovery) vs. shallow (video games). Hard work feels good.
4. Like yourself. Stay interesting.
5. Practice the "downshift"; love baseline nothingness, then everything counts (June light: 5:30 p.m., 6:30 p.m., 7:30 p.m.).
6. Love air, breeze, wind.
7. Leave shirt out (artist style but showing belly in profile) vs. tuck in and blouse to conceal?
8. Vent and get release (but be annoying to those around you) vs. hold it in check (gentleman's harness)?
9. Make your life music—let rhythm be civility,

regularity, dependability, manners, and
morality; let the melody be your personality.
10. Don't be a cynic. Be busy making value, in
spite of the milieu. Though you may not
link The cause to The effect—good causes
make good effects.

*

My father's doctor, educated Flatbush-style, so
pleased with himself—he had walked a mile to meet
my father at my flat—"the value of walking," the
strutting hen, Dr. Leifer, eighty-one then, gone
now.

*

If you write and the language has color and
tone,
accented syllables dance,
rhyme and intelligence in each refrain—
if you then call it poetry, the brain goes
numb.

Like Prince Potemkin—a war flares up in
Crimea,
the fleet sails out, he vanquishes the Turks,
the vessels swell with victory—
and the prince gets hemorrhoids.

*

The Garves Four, 2008

I do not trust my country. I firmly believe that the profit motive destroys the joy, the soul, the authenticity of every endeavor. What about these statins in my body? "What a hit these statins are and deserve to be!" my doctor said (like Michael McDonald's "What a Fool Believes"?).

Now it's twenty years later, accountability time in your daily pill. (Did LDL go out of fashion?) Do the healthy cells in my body nearby say: "Here comes the Daily Alien." It's pinpoint bombing going after the number, the cholesterol-chart-level number.

"To us healthy cells, it feels like a forced

affair." Foolish trust in big business, does it deliver a genuine life-creating product? "So knowing and intrusive, corporate shortcuts, a polluted version of what recently was only alien," say the cells.

Reclaim your trust. Invest in sweeter things. If money disappeared, what would really be left?

*

INVEST IN SWEETER THINGS. SING AGAIN.

> "The old hooty owl hooty hoots from above:
>   'Tammy's in love.' "

*

> Am I old and jaded
> Or did the world all just go flat?
> Once you were an icon if you made it.
> Now I wonder about words like that.

*

Into the tunnel of serious prep. Friday the 5th, 10:30 a.m. Don't talk no family no phone no concern. Sing easy sing more walk and sing walk more hotel room stretching sit-ups push-ups hamstrings eat light don't eat read France under Germany 1941—world fear on the day I arrived.

*

*Finishing the picture nicely is only for neatness
   freaks.
Reaching for the pith of the thing is one's true
   occupation.
And so the soul emerges. More hidden than the
   heart, so
undefined, the soul.*

THE TEXTER

I was on a stage last night in the common
age we live in. The theater crowd was restive. I
was asked to hold the start time—the earl had
not yet come. At eight minutes after, I felt for
the audience and came on. Now he strides down
quickly to his first-row seat on the center aisle.
I bring to the night a life of singing, a damaged
voice, an artist's reputation—a public display of
recovery. The earl is the town council leader,
important, all manly.

I open with a reading of mine: "I always made
peace with the fiercest of lions because I could
sing in the cage. Now I lost rapport, and stand
before one on the stage. The rude lion reaches
for blood . . ." The man we held the show up for
is a modern man. He sits nine feet before me. And
in my second song he begins to text!

I am thrown by the rules of today: Do cell
phone talkers imagine a curtain surrounds them?
Am I to disappear in the backdrop of the texting
life? I muster up good nature and peer from
the lip of the stage into the texter's lap at his

handheld thing. I smile, but it's pistols at sunrise. I
carry on singing, but I only think of him and the
next techno-spear randomly hurled from the dark.
The singing falters severely. "Scarborough Fair" is
leaden. The theater people understand—they are
called to witness the pith of my profession.

Suddenly, around the fifth song, I stop the
show and say to him, "How did you imagine I
wouldn't be completely thrown by seeing you
texting right before me?" "Because you're a
pro," he shoots back. The speed of his projected
retort tells me he's a politician. "I need to rest,"
I say, and walk off . . . I sit in the dressing room
minute after minute . . . now does the soul define
itself?

XVI

WHAT DO I THINK OF AS I WALK THESE DAYS?

I think of cholesterol. Wasn't it Tim Russert who
died of a sudden artery block near the heart?
I think of the brilliant actress I married, how
adorable she was doing "Easy Money" in her set
at Birdland last Monday. . . . I remember Paul
Simon playing poker in high school. Concealing his
emotions, he consistently won. The mind is glued
to the people we know, but the walker's home
is in the sky. All three hundred sixty degrees
of horizon. . . . There—my father's tomato plants,
how proud he was. And of his roses. He married
one. The roses grew against the cinder blocks
of our one-car garage. Twelve feet across was
the white picket fence that marked our yard
from the Skinners, Henry and Olive. I was Tom
Sawyer soon to meet Huck Finn, and my mother,
Rose, was dearer than Aunt Polly could possibly
be. As near as sunlight, I can hardly see her.
I basked within and sang with private joy. She
was the older sister after five brothers. Her hair
was frizzy, she had short fingers, workwoman's
hands. And a very beautiful face. She was the

queen of mild, in the battle blaze of my father's loud frustrations. She teared up when she grated onions and potatoes, but *Chanukah* had to have *latkes*. She ran on a mother's motor, and so it was stunning when she gave me a gift. (We just didn't do gifts in our house.) There, in white tissue, fingers so elegant, were fur-lined black leather gloves. I ran to my bedroom to cry. I was too touched. What is it all but luminous. I can't look at everything hard enough.

So I walk to see. Unglued and apart.

*

IN ALL SUCH WAYS I STRUGGLE TO BRING A LOST VOICE BACK.

My audience has grown from seventy people in Yonkers in 2013 to a thousand today. I no longer supplement my show with Q&A. The singing doesn't falter quite as much. Hitting the high notes is no longer like diving off a high board, hoping there'll be water in the pool. Now there's only an occasional death swoon. I have learned to trust in the audience's love. Displaying authentic bravery speaks for itself. Perfectionism is over. I work with smiling self-acceptance and read my "poetic bits." The new show is less is more, taken to the extreme, just Tab Laven on Martin guitar and the voice in all its nuance.

*

It's 8:10 on a Sunday morning in March. How much more do I have? I'll walk off the psychic disturbance I awoke with in this north Orlando motel. "He hopes Paul Simon will agree to a future tour." How they paint me like a fool. Last night in Ponte Vedra, I opened my show with "So I will share this room with you; and you can have this heart to break." Can they? What kind of fool am I?

Spleen. My work of recovery is about more presence in the diction, more volume, a greater being in my being, a higher leap of faith. Tonight I will play a show in Palm Beach Gardens—no. 65 since returning to the stage last year, all filled with fear and exaltation. I miss my family's sweet embrace. Sunday night is Oscars. Monday, *New York* magazine. Should I cancel the makeup appointment? I'd like to avoid being done to. No driver to the shoot? I could walk there and sing in the street—call my soul my own and hope for retouching.

*

We're all in the throes of greater volatility.
What are we sending up into the air?
Is it *largo* turned to *allegro*
   or a dance of interaction in a frenzy
      everywhere?

I walked across the Appalachians,
Perfect undulations, ambler's waves of joy;
Ridge to ridge—four and a half miles,
    terrestrial corduroy.

Weather is whatever;
It never levels off.
If it peaks at two in Pennsylvania,
    at four-fifteen, it lies in a West Virginian
        trough.

*

Forget not, lest ye be forgotten. Forgive, or
remain unforgiven.

*

25 RECORDS IN THE ORDER THEY CHANGED MY LIFE

1) Enrico Caruso	Aria from *The Pearl Fishers*
2) The Andrews Sisters	"Rum and Coca-Cola"
3) Nat King Cole	"Too Young"
4) Nat King Cole	"Nature Boy"
5) *Carousel*, the show	"If I Loved You"
6) Bing Crosby	"White Christmas"
7) The Crew Cuts	"Sh-Boom"
8) Frankie Ford	"Sea Cruise"
9) Huey "Piano" Smith	"Don't Ya Just Know It"
10) Sam Cooke	"You Send Me"
11) The Everly Brothers	*Songs Our Daddy Taught Us* (LP)

12) Johnny Mathis	"It's Not for Me to Say"
13) Ike and Tina Turner	"River Deep-Mountain High"
14) The Righteous Brothers	"Ol' Man River"
15) The Beatles	"Here, There and Everywhere"
16) The Beach Boys	"Good Vibrations"
17) The Swingle Singers	*Jazz Sebastian Bach* (LP)
18) The Hi-Lo's	*Suddenly It's the Hi-Lo's*
19) Simon and Garfunkel	"Scarborough Fair"
20) Joan Baez	*Joan Baez* (LP)
21) J. S. Bach	*The Christmas Oratorio* (3 LPs)
22) Lenny Bruce	*American* (LP), "Frank Dell"
23) Nichols & May	*Nichols & May Examine Doctors* (LP)
24) Steve Reich	*Music for 18 Musicians* (LP)
25) Chet Baker	any vocal

*

War is not the answer; for only love can conquer hate.

—Marvin Gaye, "What's Going On"

*

**A Turkish worker, seeing my arms out wide,
Hugs me for the embrace.**

*

The first thing you see is the other man's
        point of view.
I dust off the earth, the dance is done,
    the seat of my pants don't matter none . . .
There's Laurie, there's Steve, there's everyone—
    was I too forgiving? I saw it all as true—
        what man does, and how funny it was
        what I did too . . .

O Earth you are too wonderful for anyone
        to see.
And blindest of all was me.

*

The heart pushes wider; there is joy!
    Dear Sandy, Perhaps we've been exclusive with
our love. The fifty-four years of our friendship
are a construct. Is it constricting? Did Jonathan
and David own a puppy?
    Now you are released from the first seventy-
one, and I from the singing choir. Now we turn
in the widening gyre. Embracing human dignity
still, we open our arms to our beautiful women,
to Jerry Speyer, to come what will, your sister
Ruth, to our boys, to both of our blindness, to
Jack and Rose, Sarah and Carl, l'chaim.
    Songs were ours to sing and we have sung
them; stars shone down on us and now we swim
among them.

*

There was a moment I noted in the dressing
room in Milwaukee. It was winter turning spring.
Thursday, March the twentieth, seven-seventeen,
eight o'clock show. The vernal equinox. I strained
to feel our planet tilting neither toward nor away
from the sun. The night was fifty months since
I lost my voice. And on that fifteen hundred
and nineteenth night, THE VOICE RETURNED IN FULL.'
2014. In Chicago, two nights later, the seventieth
show of recovery, stage legs returned, spring was
here. I could sing again.

*

When I was young I was Achilles.
It was excellence, honor, bravery
    and blood all played out on
        the stage of the world.

Now I am Odysseus, a voyager,
    a traveler for travel's sake.
As if something was forgotten,
    I go east.
The star of the play now is the
    earth itself, Ireland to Istanbul.
In the Beginning and at the End
    there was Light.
The beauty of light finds a room
    in us—what is it all but luminous?

*

The journalist came today. Pragmatic meets poetic. She came to "cover my walk." Steak and cheese. Turkey au gratin. The Getter meets the Gotten. She got me coming through Tekirdag. We walked along the Sea of Marmara, next to the Ottoman traffic—German inquisition, rambling Turkish taffy. Alive and on display, how can I convey to her my trek of speckled radiance, this tour of a million magnificent steps?

My Constantinople is colorful. Perhaps her beige bison is tan bull.

*

THE DEATH OF MIKE NICHOLS

Life will be different for us now. Mike Nichols is not alive. He was the most sparkling man among us. The self is a creation. Mike created an extraordinary star—so bright, so extremely clever—himself. When you were with him, he brought you up to your best smart self, and kept it light and funny. To act for him on camera was to glide on a liquid film of intelligence. Before each scene, Mike gave his actors a truly brilliant and subversive insight into the scene. As you were stirred, he then joked, you laughed, he walked away, and said, "Roll camera." Now that he has truly walked away, the act of life is, for me, forever charmed.

*

EuroWalk completed! Leg #30. Ipsala to Istanbul. I walk because I'm fiercely in love with being alive. I walk for the lungs to exhale and expel. I walk for the spine to be upright. I walk to hear the rooster. I am a Singer.

I love to see decrepit things—history, old shacks. The beauty of six o'clock, of seven, of eight, the twilit lay of the land in lullaby. I play with mathematics. I calibrate. Lately I enjoy guessing the steps to the mosque up ahead. Every two steps is a five-foot pace; a hundred meters, sixty-eight of them, is a short home run.

Most of all I walk to relax, a word that means the world to me, a door to everything I care about. The life within. Philosophy. The beauty behind the beauty—*Shibooli*. So I remember, I measure, I miss my loves at home. I empty out to come about. I am a Singer.

*

After Laurie died, nights began to feel sadder
    than days.
Going on the road for shows had an aching
    lonesome
    check-in time in strange hotels at night.
Where am I?
Why?

I am spinning in black, longing for love, for
    the sun, for
Showtime!

*

Then some things are so easy to remember—
September 19, 1981, our CONCERT IN CENTRAL
PARK. . . . All the band guys on stage around me.
Pete Carr on guitar at my right. The sky cleared
at five; the buzz around town was palpable,
growing fast. I see masses of people, beyond
the Great Lawn, under the trees. The wheel of
fortune had spun to our slot. Now go to work:
listen intently, blend the voices, match the texture,
mix the volumes (little 64ths of an inch from the
mic), breathe along with your childhood friend . . .

   We were front-page news of the *New York
Times* next day. I voted myself a C+ as I walked
offstage.

   —We blew it. (I wanted the nuances finer, more
controlled.)

   —Are you crazy, Artie?

With Luis Perelman, architecture schoolmate, in front
of the Plaza Hotel in New York City, c. 1963

XVII

When I was twenty-three, in architecture school, my classmate Luis, follower of Gurdjieff, invited me to his Saturday night party. "There'll be smoking," he whispered.

We met at his narrow brownstone on the topmost floor. His father, a psychiatrist, met his wealthy clients down below. The Rock Church was just next door. In those fabulous stoned Saturday nights, we passed a piece of reefer around in a circle of four and they ended with Sunday morning gospel singing from the church next door. Such a nice Manhattan scene. I had to bring my friend Paul Simon into it. We used the apartment as a rehearsal place for our first Columbia album. No drugs. This was the "cool" we lived within. We knew how to do "Sparrow" from the summer of working English folk clubs, but now it was "Benedictus." These were the Kennedy years.

*

We die incrementally. The lungs lose breath in increments. My baby learned sadness from his parents, fight by fight. Little murders every

day. Why can't I button the cuffs of my shirt?
Identity dying. Fingerprints wearing away.

*

The man who gave his life to you.
My meager self remains,
Witness to bereavement
And winding sheets with bloodstains.

Bold achievements bound in chains
Acted on your stage;
My written book is yours to keep
My cold hand writes the index page.

All's asleep in camouflage,
Spring became a November tree.
Bitter pears are ripening
In authenticity.

*

I sang for a thousand Parisians last night and did
my ninety-minute set. In the year 2015, I haven't
finished yet. At dinner with the promoter, after
the wonderful show within a golden Rembrandt
frame, sits the portrait of the artist we know.
But I know his recent awakening . . .
    Paris—so warm to an American? I feel the room
to grow. I see the buds of the croci—somethin's
comin'.

*

Sometimes life is an unmitigated joy. James is Arthur Junior now. He's twenty-four. The thrust of his argument is taking place in the wholeness of man. He sang onstage in my Tokyo show two months ago. With arms around each other's waist we finished "Let It Be Me"—"So never leave me lonely, tell me you love me only. And that you'll always—let it be me." Then he kissed me on the neck, with a full embrace. The audience witnessed a father's plea, and a son raised and bathed in love. Under the applause, I put in his ear: "This could be the finest moment." . . . Miracles thread through a singer's life.

*

And finally one more shop—jewelers, flowers—then bookshop (can I humbly make my entry?) Can Sandy Greenberg, who's been sightless since college (glaucoma set in in our sophomore yr.) lead us all toward the end of blindness by 2020? Will the global divide of 2015, along religious lines, so bloody and tragic, find a bridge?

ART GARFUNKEL AT CARNEGIE HALL—
OCTOBER 3, 2015

Dear Todd,

I had a home run last night in New York City—sold out up to the rafters. I was in form. My love showed. Stage legs are back. Less is more worked beautifully in the room.

Two Great Artists (Garfunkel
and Steve Gadd)

Little Beau started the night with intense
adorability. In his rented tuxedo, "Ladies and
Gentlemen, here's my Daddy." I open with "April
Come She Will," then give them my piece, 3 Stages
of the Fame Trip. 3rd stage—poor Domino, booked
to work a five-year-old's birthday party, and he's

Beau Daniel Garfunkel, age nine

lame. Now I walk forward. "I AM Domino" (I slip into the voice of Dylan Thomas). "I wasn't always this way; I was once a lovely little curly-headed lad. . . . Now I'm an old entertainer with a phony British accent. But the heart is young. And the voice is back." Surge into "The Boxer."

Will my personal identity emerge in these final pages? I look over the hill for Arthur.

"I dare to be a man who loves pretty things—purple magenta, dusty rose . . . here's 'Perfect

Moment,' a song I co-wrote and put into the eleventh of my twelve solo albums." Then I read my piece "Beau and the Globe" (bliss in the home life). I sang "A Heart in New York" / "All I Know." The voice is firm, I'm on tonight.

Little Beau has begun to play the harp. What could be more divine?

I give them "The Texter," my story of vocal vulnerability. When I get to the part where I walk off.', the Carnegie audience applauds me. "Ahh," I say, "you applaud confrontation . . . but where, exactly, do you go from there?"

After my bit on Nicholson, I do "Scarborough Fair" and never-before-heard "Side of a Hill," the antiwar song tucked between the lines of Scarborough. Then the galloping "Poem on the Underground Wall," and the first half ends.

Tonight I will do the Jimmy Fallon *Tonight Show*, and hope to sell tickets for this Saturday night's Carnegie Hall show, where you practice, practice to get there. I practiced last week at the Royal Albert Hall in London. Junior joined me with "Let It Be Me."

My brother Jerome sells *The Singer* in the lobby. After the intermission, Arthur and I came out together. I say, "This is my son, I want you to hear him sing." We duet "Devoted to You." I leave. He solos "Smile." He absolutely kills; the finishing notes are an octave higher than his father's range.!!

I then read my "Note to Self"; CBS-TV wanted me to give my "life lessons," I say. "What do we really ever learn about life, except that it's a fabulous mystery, and you have to be kind to people? Fame is a kick—the party's at your house. Then if you can embrace the differentness of another . . ." Into "Homeward Bound," then Randy Newman's "Real Emotional Girl" (work that stage, left and right), and the piece about my father, who gave me Enrico Caruso. It led to "Bridge Over Troubled Water." I was five.

> **"A fallen leaf blown through the grass." It was Mike Nichols who inspired my piece "important lives will end."**

And my life—a piece of work or a piece of nothing? I sing the most delicate "For Emily," then a prose poem of mine: "I have sung for creatures all my life—humans in '51." I illustrate a Hebrew piece, a lovely minor-key memory. . . . "Years later, I sang for cows. As I walked the country . . . I get weary and sick of tryin', I'm tired of livin'," I sing. "Many eyes widen, one creature's cryin'," I say. "I'm feared of dyin'," I sing with fragility. (Who says this in a pop performance, Todd?) Then into blue-lit "Bright Eyes."

Now Paul Simon, "Who will speak at whose funeral?"(Jack Benny deadpan pause.)

I wait for the final blank page to come over
the bridge and write me—tell me what
this life amounts to. Is it a syncline?

"The Sound of Silence." When the drum track
kicks into the second verse, we go rock 'n' roll.
Fade to black. Bows. Great mutual appreciation.

Love is all there is.

At the gathering after the triumph onstage,
I see my foolish pictures taken. There—the age;
eyeliner extended. What kind of fool am I?

Who could stick by this man?

Tab Laven and I do "Kathy's Song," the most
beautiful singing of the night. Arthur Jr. returns,
tribute to Phil Everly, "Let It Be Me." Cheek
to cheek, I sing to my boy, "So never leave me
lonely." His warmth, so palpable, Kim runs on,
roses for us. "This is my bride, the great actress
Kathryn Luce." We kiss.

Somehow, in a miracle of faith, it is my
Kathryn, my Kim. She threw a party for
me that was my life.

I introduce "Bridge" with my bit about playing
the Albert Hall. Soon I will rise onto the mesa.
Enter the pop warrior. . . . Be beautiful, be a
man. . . . Go out on the field of praise to the

Onstage at Carnegie Hall

apron, tell every stall. . . . Tonight is all. . . .
When you're weary, feelin' small. We do verses,
then out. Thunderous applause—the syncline.

**But before the party, onstage, I finished as
usual, hand on heart.**

I leave. Return with thank God "for allowing
me to be the conduit." "Now I Lay Me Down to
Sleep." Softly, at the end: "Goodnight, New York."
Bows of deep gratitude.

Now I belong to the back of the balcony.

Beau about to pull my sleeve to leave. *I threw
it all to the upper deck.*

Acknowledgments

For three and a half decades I have been
following inspiration as it led me onto the page.
Then Dan Strone of Trident Media told me:
"You might have a book here." (He especially
liked that it was all handwritten.) I was absolutely
thrilled when the great publishing house of
Alfred A. Knopf accepted my writing. (Maybe
my unusual book *does* communicate.) I started
working with legendary editor Vicky Wilson. I
was her student in Bookland. Thank you sincerely,
Victoria, for your empathy. My thanks go to
Ryan Smernoff at Knopf. Since God is in the
details, his guiding of me to publication was godly.
And my deepest thanks to Sandy Greenberg for
his beautiful judgment.

Photographic Credits

All of the images in this book are from the author's personal archives, with the exceptions listed below:

page 27   © Bob Gruen

page 33   © Moviestore collection Ltd / Alamy Stock Photo

page 43   © Margaret Herrick Library/Academy of Motion Picture Arts and Sciences, courtesy of Gayle Simon

page 44   © Jim Marshall Photography LLC

page 52   Photograph courtesy of Gayle Simon

page 61   Photograph by Stanislav Traykov, courtesy of Wikimedia Commons

pages 64, 69, 83, 97, 104, 108, 124, 142, 168, 197, 198, 208, 216   © Linda Mahon

page 119   © Tricia Lewis

page 241   © Gil Cohen Magen / AFP / Getty Images